Y0-AIX-114

DISCARDED

THE WORKS OF JAMES WHITCOMB RILEY
VOL. VI.

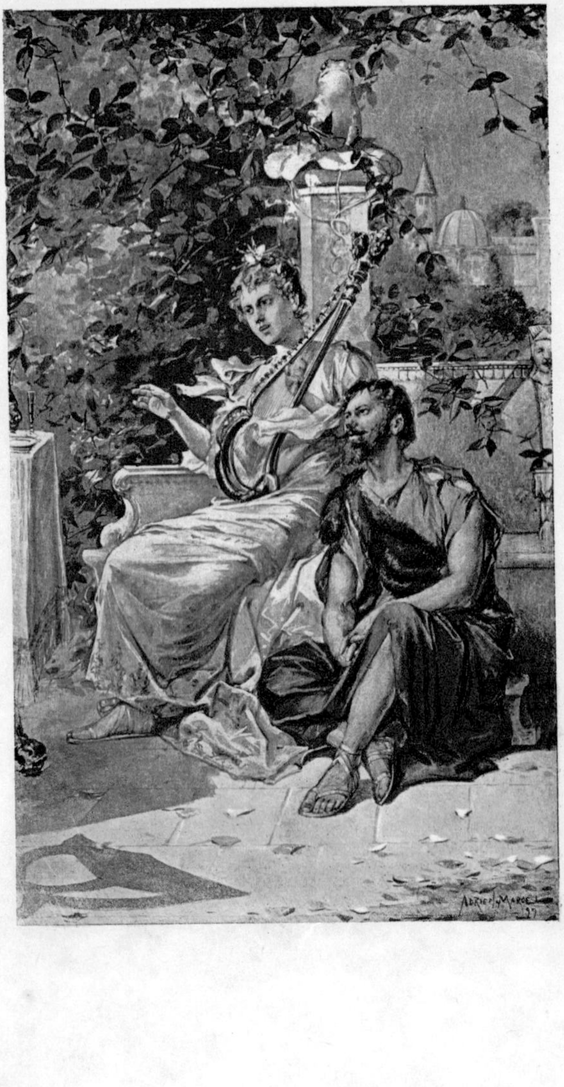

THE POEMS AND PROSE
❧ ❧ SKETCHES OF ❧ ❧
JAMES WHITCOMB RILEY

THE FLYING ISLANDS
OF THE NIGHT ❦ ❦ ❦

CHARLES SCRIBNER'S
SONS ❦ NEW YORK ❦ 1906

Copyright, 1891, 1898, by
JAMES WHITCOMB RILEY

₊ *The publication of this Homestead Edition of the works
of James Whitcomb Riley is made possible by the
courtesy of The Bowen-Merrill Company, of Indianapolis, the original publishers of Mr. Riley's books.*

TO
MADISON CAWEIN

CONTENTS

	PAGE
THE FLYING ISLANDS OF THE NIGHT	1
For the Song's sake; even so	3
SPIRK AND WUNK RHYMES — ROUNDS AND CATCHES	
To loll back, in a misty hammock, swung	114
THE LOVELY HUSBAND	116
THE LIGHT OF LOVE	120
SONGS TUNELESS	121
OUT OF THE DARK AND THE DEARTH	124
SPIRK TROLL-DERISIVE	125
THE ROMAUNT OF KING MORDAMEER	127
DEATH	133
WE ARE NOT ALWAYS GLAD WHEN WE SMILE	135
THE WEREWIFE	137
THE RAIN	139
FOR YOU	140
THE STRANGE YOUNG MAN	142
"DREAM"	145
A WRANGDILLION	147

CONTENTS

	PAGE
THE WITCH OF ERKMURDEN	149
LAUGHTER	153
ERE I WENT MAD	154
ETERNITY	157
THE SPEEDING OF THE KING'S SPITE	158
THE ASSASSIN	165
A VARIATION	166
AN OUT-WORN SAPPHO	169
AFTER DEATH	175
TO THE WINE-GOD MERLUS	177
THE QUEST	178
SONG OF PARTING	180
THREE SEVERAL BIRDS	182

THE FLYING ISLANDS OF THE NIGHT

" A thynge of wytchencreft—an idle dreme."

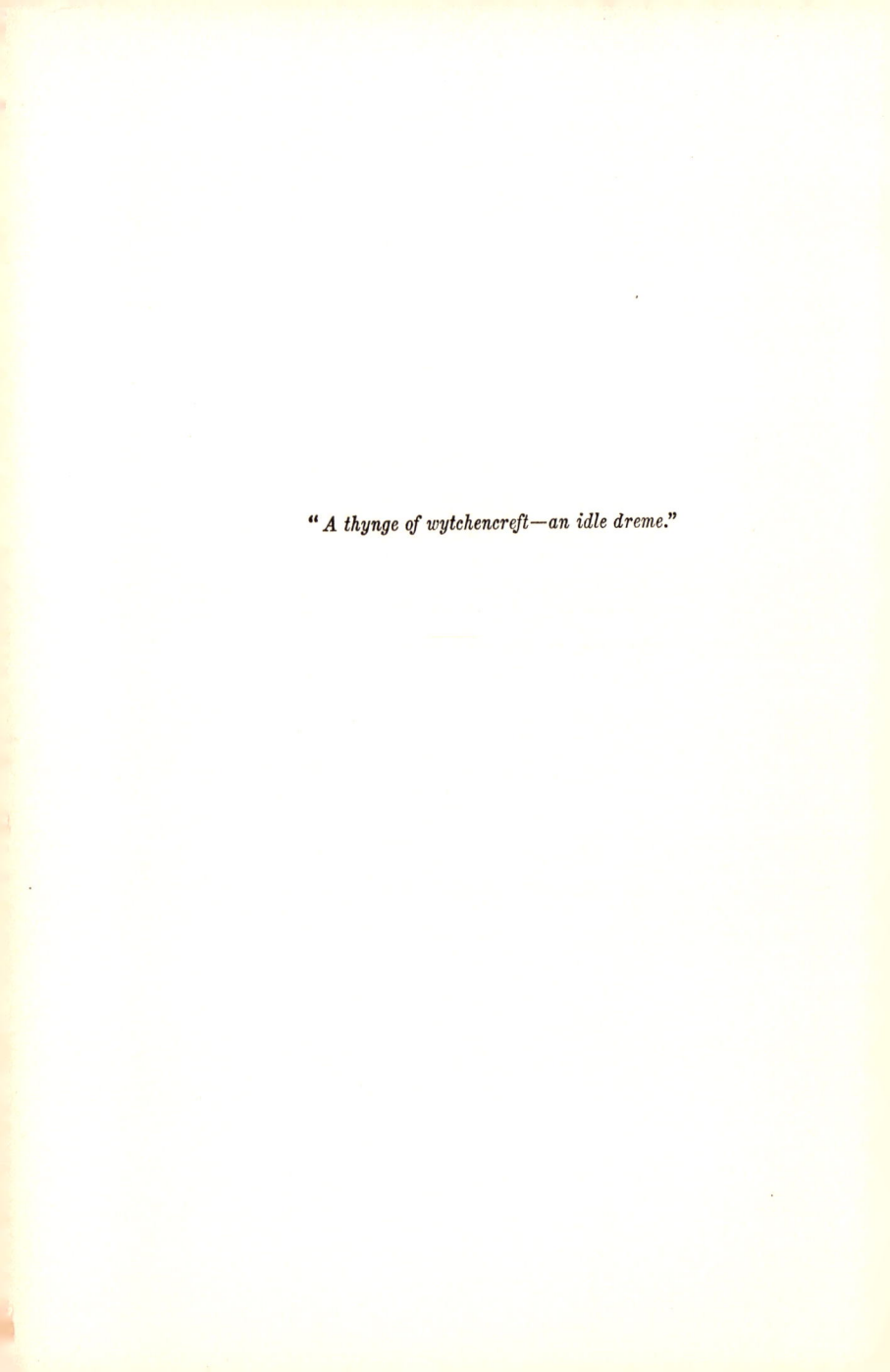

FOR the Song's sake; even so:
Humor it, and let it go
All untamed and wild of wing—
Leave it ever truanting.

> *Be its flight elusive!—Lo,*
> *For the Song's sake—even so.—*
> *Yield it but an ear as kind*
> *As thou perkest to the wind.*

Who will name us what the seas
Have sung on for centuries?
For the Song's sake! Even so—
Sing, O Seas! and Breezes, blow!

> *Sing! or Wave or Wind or Bird—*
> *Sing! nor ever afterward*
> *Clear thy meaning to us—No!—*
> *For the Song's sake. Even so.*

DRAMATIS PERSONÆ

KRUNG	King—*of the* Spirks.
CRESTILLOMEEM	*The* Queen—*Second Consort to* Krung.
SPRAIVOLL	*The* Tune-Fool.
AMPHINE	Prince—*Son of* Krung.
DWAINIE	*A* Princess—*of the* Wunks.
JUCKLET	*A* Dwarf—*of the* Spirks.
CREECH *and* GRITCHFANG	Nightmares

Counsellors, Courtiers, Heralds, etc., etc., etc.

THE FLYING ISLANDS OF THE NIGHT

ACT I.

SCENE—THE FLYING ISLANDS.

SCENE I. Spirkland. *Time, Moondawn. Interior Court of* KRUNG. *A vast, pendent star burns dimly in dome above throne.* CRESTILLOMEEM *discovered languidly reclining at foot of empty throne, an overturned goblet lying near, as though just drained. The* Queen, *in seeming dazed, ecstatic state, raptly gazing upward, listening. Swarming forms and features in air above, seen eerily coming and going, blending and intermingling in domed ceiling-spaces of court. Weird music. Mystic, luminous, beautiful faces detached from swarm, float, singly, forward,—tremulously, and in succession, poising in mid-air and chanting.*

FIRST FACE.

And who hath known her—like as *I*
Have known her?—since the envying sky
Filched from her cheeks its morning-hue,
And from her eyes its glory, too,
Of dazzling shine and diamond-dew.

SECOND FACE.

I knew her—long and long before
High Æo loosed her palm and thought:
"What awful splendor have I wrought
To dazzle earth and Heaven, too!"

THIRD FACE.

I knew her—long ere Night was o'er—
Ere Æo yet conjectured what
To fashion Day of—ay, before
He sprinkled stars across the floor
Of dark, and swept that form of mine,
E'en as a fleck of blinded shine,
Back to the black where light was not.

THE FLYING ISLANDS OF THE NIGHT

Fourth Face.

Ere day was dreamt, I saw her face
Lift from some starry hiding-place
Where our old moon was kneeling while
She lit its features with her smile.

Fifth Face.

I knew her while these islands yet
Were nestlings—ere they feathered wing,
Or e'en could gape with them or get
Apoise the laziest-ambling breeze,
Or cheep, chirp out, or anything!
When Time crooned rhymes of nurseries
Above them—nodded, dozed and slept,
And knew it not, till, wakening,
The morning-stars agreed to sing
And Heaven's first tender dews were wept.

Sixth Face.

I knew her when the jealous hands
Of Angels set her sculptured form
Upon a pedestal of storm

And let her to this land with strands
Of twisted lightnings.

        SEVENTH FACE.

              And I heard
Her voice ere she could tone a word
Of any but the Seraph-tongue.—
And O sad-sweeter than all sung-
Or word-said things!—to hear her say,
Between the tears she dashed away:—
"Lo, launched from the offended sight
Of Æo!—anguish infinite
Is ours, O Sisterhood of Sin!
Yet is thy service mine by right,
And, sweet as I may rule it, thus
Shall Sin's myrrh-savor taste to us—
Sin's Empress—let my reign begin!"

    CHORUS OF SWARMING FACES.

We follow thee forever on!
Thro' darkest night and dimmest dawn;

Thro' storm and calm—thro' shower and shine,
Hear thou our voices answering thine:
>   We follow—*craving* but to be
>   Thy followers.—We follow thee—
>   We follow, follow, follow thee!

We follow ever on and on—
O'er hill and hollow, brake and lawn;
Thro' grewsome vale and dread ravine
Where light of day is never seen.—
>   We waver not in loyalty,—
>   Unfaltering we follow thee—
>   We follow, follow, follow thee!

We follow ever on and on!
The shroud of night around us drawn,
Though wet with mists, is wild-ashine
With stars to light that path of thine;—
>   The glow-worms, too, befriend us—we
>   Shall fail not as we follow thee.
>   We follow, follow, follow thee!

We follow ever on and on.—
The notchèd reeds we pipe upon
Are pithed with music, keener blown
And blither where thou leadest lone—
      Glad pangs of its ecstatic glee
      Shall reach thee as we follow thee.
      We follow, follow, follow thee!

We follow ever on and on:
We know the ways thy feet have gone,—
The grass is greener, and the bloom
Of roses richer in perfume—
      And birds of every blooming tree
      Sing sweeter as we follow thee.
      We follow, follow, **follow** thee!

We follow ever on and on;
For wheresoever thou **hast** gone
We hasten joyous, knowing there
Is sweeter sin than otherwhere—
      Leave still its latest cup, that we
      May drain it as we follow thee.
      We follow, follow, **follow thee!**

[*Throughout final stanzas, faces in fore- and forms in background slowly vanish, and voices gradually fail to sheer silence.*—CRESTILLOMEEM, *rising, and wistfully gazing and listening; then, evidently regaining wonted self, looks to be assured of being wholly alone—then speaks.*]

CRESTILLOMEEM.

The Throne is throwing wide its gilded arms
To welcome me. The Throne of Krung! Ha! ha!
Leap up, ye lazy echoes, and laugh loud!
For I, Crestillomeem, the Queen—ha! ha!
Do fling my richest mirth into your mouths
That ye may fatten ripe with mockery!
I marvel what the kingdom would become
Were I not here to nurse it like a babe
And dandle it above the reach and clutch
Of intermeddlers in the royal line
And their attendant serfs. *Ho!* Jucklet, ho!
'Tis time my knarlèd warp of nice anatomy
Were here, to weave us on upon our mesh
Of silken villanies. *Ho!* Jucklet, ho!

[*Lifts secret door in pave and drops a star-bud through opening. Enter* JUCKLET *from below.*]

JUCKLET.

Spang sprit! my gracious Queen! but thou hast scorched
My left ear to a cinder! and my head
Rings like a ding-dong on the coast of death!
For, patient hate! thy hasty signal burst
Full in my face as hitherward I came!
But though my lug be fried to crisp, and my
Singed wig stinks like a little sun-stewed Wunk,
I stretch my fragrant presence at thy feet
And kiss thy sandal with a blistered lip.

CRESTILLOMEEM.

Hold! rare-done fool, lest I may bid the cook
To bake thee brown! How fares the King by this?

JUCKLET.

Save couched midmost his lordly hoard of books,
I left him sleeping like a quinsied babe

THE FLYING ISLANDS OF THE NIGHT

Next the guest-chamber of a poor man's house:
But ere I came away, to rest mine ears,
I salved his welded lids, uncorked his nose,
And o'er the odorous blossom of his lips
Re-squeezed the tinctured sponge, and felt his pulse
Come staggering back to regularity.
And four hours hence his Highness will awake
And *Peace* will take a nap!

CRESTILLOMEEM.

Ha! What mean you?

JUCKLET. [*Ominously.*]

I mean that he suspects our knaveries.—
Some covert spy is burrowed in the court—
Nay, and I pray thee startle not *aloud*,
But mute thy very heart in its out-throb,
And let the blanching of thy cheeks but be
A whispering sort of pallor!

CRESTILLOMEEM.

A spy?—Here?

JUCKLET.

Ay, *here*—and haply even *now*. And one
Whose unseen eye seems ever focussed keen
Upon our action, and whose hungering ear
Eats every crumb of counsel that we drop
In these our secret interviews!—For he—
The King—through all his talking-sleep to-day
Hath jabbered of intrigue, conspiracy—
Of treachery and hate in fellowship,
With dire designs upon his royal bulk,
To oust it from the Throne.

CRESTILLOMEEM.

                He spake my name?

JUCKLET.

O Queen, he speaks not ever but thy name
Makes melody of every sentence.—Yea,
He thinks thee even true to him as thou
Art fickle, false and subtle! O how blind
And lame, and deaf and dumb, and worn and weak,

And faint, and sick, and all-commodious
His dear love is! In sooth, O wifely one,
Thy malleable spouse doth mind me of
That pliant hero of the bald old catch
"The Lovely Husband."—Shall I wreak the thing?

[*Sings—with much affected gravity and grimace.*]

> O a lovely husband he was known,
> He loved his wife and her a-lone;
> She reaped the harvest he had sown;
> She ate the meat; he picked the bone.
>> With mixed admirers every size,
>> She smiled on each without disguise;
>> This lovely husband closed his eyes
>> Lest he might take her by surprise.

[*Aside, exclamatory.*]

Chorious uproarious!

[*Then pantomime as though pulling at bell-rope—
singing in pent, explosive utterance.*]

Trot!
> Run!
>> Wasn't he a handy hubby?

What
> Fun
>> She could plot and plan!

Not
> **One**
>> Other such a dandy hubby
>> As this lovely man!

> CRESTILLOMEEM.

Or talk or tune, wilt thou wind up thy tongue
Nor let it tangle in a knot of words!
What said the King?

> JUCKLET. [*With recovered reverence.*]

>> He said: "Crestillomeem—
O that *she* knew this thick distress of mine!—
Her counsel would *anoint* me and her voice
Would flow in limpid wisdom o'er my woes

And, like a love-balm, lave my secret grief
And lull my sleepless heart!" [*Aside*] And so went on,
Struggling all maudlin in the wrangled web
That well-nigh hath cocooned him!

CRESTILLOMEEM.

Did he yield
No hint of this mysterious distress
He needs must hold sequestered from his Queen?
What said he in his talking-sleep by which
Some clew were gained of how and when and whence
His trouble came?

JUCKLET.

In one strange phase he spake
As though some sprited lady talked with him.—
Full courteously he said: "In woman's guise
Thou comest, yet I think thou art, in sooth,
But woman in thy form.—Thy words are strange
And leave me mystified. I feel the truth
Of all thou hast declared, and yet so vague
And shadow-like thy meaning is to me,

I know not how to act to ward the blow
Thou sayest is hanging o'er me even now."
And then, with open hands held pleadingly,
He asked, "Who *is* my foe?"—And o'er his face
A sudden pallor flashed, like death itself,
As though, if answer had been given, it
Had fallen like a curse.

Crestillomeem.

                I'll stake my soul
Thrice over in the grinning teeth of doom,
'Tis Dwainie of the Wunks who peeks and peers
With those fine eyes of hers in our affairs
And carries Krung, in some disguise, these hints
Of our intent! See thou that silence falls
Forever on her lips, and that the sight
She wastes upon our secret action blurs
With gray and grisly skum that shall for aye
Conceal us from her gaze while she writhes blind
And fangless as the fat worms of the grave!
Here! take this tuft of downy druze, and when

Thou comest on her, fronting full and fair,
Say "*Sherzham!*" thrice, and fluff it in her face.

JUCKLET.

Thou knowest scanty magic, O my Queen,
But all thou dost is fairly excellent—
An *this* charm work, thou shalt have fuller faith
Than still I must withhold.

  [*Takes charm, with extravagant salutation.*]

CRESTILLOMEEM.

Thou gibing knave!
Thou thing! Dost dare to name my sorcery
As any trifling gift? Behold what might
Be thine an thy deserving wavered not
In stable and abiding service to
Thy Queen!

[*She presses suddenly her palm upon his eyes, then lifts her
    softly opening hand upward, his gaze following, where,
    slowly shaping in the air above them, appears sem-
    blance—or counter-self—of* CRESTILLOMEEM, *clothed in*

most radiant youth, her maiden-face bent downward to a moon-lit sward, where kneels a lover-knight—flawless in manly symmetry and princely beauty,—yet none other than the counter-self of JUCKLET, *eeriely and with strange sweetness singing, to some curiously tinkling instrument, the praises of its queenly mistress:* JUCKLET *and* CRESTILLOMEEM *transfixed below—trancedly gazing on their mystic selves above.*]

SEMBLANCE OF JUCKLET. [*Sings.*]

Crestillomeem !

   Crestillomeem !
Soul of my slumber!—Dream of my dream !
Moonlight may fall not as goldenly fair
As falls the gold of thine opulent hair—
Nay, nor the starlight as dazzlingly gleam
As gleam thine eyes, 'Mecma— Crestillomeem !—
  Stars of the skies, 'Meema—

    Crestillomeem !

SEMBLANCE OF CRESTILLOMEEM. [*Sings.*]

O Prince divine!

       O Prince divine!
Tempt thou me not with that sweet voice of thine!
Though my proud brow bear the blaze of a crown,
Lo, at thy feet must its glory bow down,
That from the dust thou mayest lift me to shine
Heaven'd in thy heart's rapture, O Prince divine!—
    Queen of thy love ever,

          O Prince divine!

SEMBLANCE OF JUCKLET. [*Sings.*]

Crestillomeem!

      Crestillomeem!
Our life shall flow as a musical stream—
Windingly—placidly on shall it wend,
Marged with mazhoora-bloom banks without end—
Word-birds shall call thee and dreamily scream,
" Where dost thou cruise, 'Meema—Crestillomeem?
    Whither away, 'Meema?—

         Crestillomeem!"

DUO.

[*Vision and voices gradually failing away.*]

Crestillomeem!

Crestillomeem!
Soul of my slumber!—Dream of my dream!
Star of Love's light, 'Meema—Crestillomeem!
Crescent of Night, 'Meema!—
Crestillomeem!

[*With song, vision likewise fails utterly.*]

CRESTILLOMEEM.

[*To* JUCKLET, *still trancedly staring upward.*]

How now, thou clabber-brainèd spudge!—
Thou squelk!—thou—

JUCKLET.

Nay, O Queen! contort me not
To more condensèd littleness than now
My shamèd frame incurreth on itself,

THE FLYING ISLANDS OF THE NIGHT

Seeing what might fare with it, didst *thou* will
Kindly to nip it with thy magic *here*
And leave it living in that form i' the air,
Forever pranking o'er the daisied sward
In wake of sandal-prints that dint the dews
As lightly as, in thy late maidenhood,
Thine own must needs have done in flighting from
The dread encroachments of the King.

CRESTILLOMEEM.

Nay—peace!

JUCKLET.

So be it, O sweet Mystic.—But I crave
One service of thy magic yet.—*Amphine!*—
Breed me some special, damnèd philter for
Amphine—the *fair* Amphine!—to chuck it him,
Some serenade-tide, in a sodden slug
O' pastry, 'twixt the door-crack and a screech
O' rusty hinges.—Hey! Amphine, the *fair!*—
And let me, too, elect his doom, O Queen!—

Listed against thee, he, too, doubtless hath
Been favored with an outline of our scheme.—
And I would kick my soul all over hell
If I might juggle his fine figure up
In such a shape as mine!

CRESTILLOMEEM.

Then this:—When thou
Canst come upon him bent above a flower,
Or any blooming thing, and thou, arear,
Shalt reach it first and, thwartwise, touch it fair,
And with thy knuckle flick him on the knee,—
Then—his fine form will shrink and shrivel up
As warty as a toad's—so hideous,
Thine own shall seem a marvel of rare grace!
Though idly speak'st thou of my mystic skill,
'Twas that which won the King for me;—'twas that
Bereft him of his daughter ere we had
Been wedded yet a haed:—She strangely went
Astray one moonset from the palace-steps—
She went—nor yet returned.—Was it not strange?—

She would be wedded to an alien prince
The morrow midnight—to a prince whose sire
I once knew, in lost hours of lute and song,
When *he* was but a prince—*I* but a mouth
For him to lift up sippingly and drain
To lees most ultimate of stammering sobs
And maudlin wanderings of blinded breath.

JUCKLET. [*Aside.*]

Twigg-brebblets! but her Majesty hath speech
That doth bejuice all metaphor to drip
And spray and mist of sweetness!

CRESTILLOMEEM. [*Confusedly.*]

Where was I?
O, ay!—The princess went—she strangely went!—
E'en as I deemed her lover-princeling would
As strangely go, were she not soon restored.—
As so he did:—That airy penalty
The jocund Fates provide our love-lorn wights
In this glad island: So for thrice three nights
They spun the prince his line and marked him pay

It out (despite all warnings of his doom)
In fast and sleepless search for her—and *then*
They tripped his fumbling feet and he fell—UP!—
Up!—as 'tis writ—sheer past Heaven's flinching walls
And topmost cornices.—Up—up and on!—
And, it is grimly guessed of those who thus
For such a term bemoan an absent love,
And so fall *up*wise, they must needs fall on—
And on and on—and on—and on—and on!
Ha! ha!

JUCKLET.

Quahh! but the prince's holden breath
Must ache his throat by this! But, O my Queen,
What of the princess?—and—

CRESTILLOMEEM.

The princess?—Ay—
The princess! Ay, she went—she strangely went!
And when the dainty vagrant came not back—
Both sire and son in apprehensive throes
Of royal grief—the very Throne befogged

THE FLYING ISLANDS OF THE NIGHT

In sighs and tears!—when all hope waned at last,
And all the spies of Spirkland, in her quest,
Came straggling empty-handed home again,—
Why, then the wise King sleeved his rainy eyes
And sagely thought the pretty princess had
Strayed to the island's edge and tumbled off.
I could have set his mind at ease on that—
I could have told him,—*yea*, she tumbled off—
I tumbled her!—and tumbled her so plump,
She tumbled in an under-island, then
Just slow-unmooring from our own and poised
For unknown voyagings of flight afar
And all remote of latitudes of ours.—
Ay, into that land I tumbled her from which
But one charm known to art can tumble her
Back into this,—and *that* charm (guilt be praised!)
Is lodged not in the wit nor the desire
Of my rare lore.

JUCKLET.

Thereinasmuch find joy!
But dost thou know that rumors flutter now

Among thy subjects of thy sorceries?—
The art being *banned*, thou knowest; or, unhoused,
Is unleashed pitilessly by the grim,
Facetious body of the dridular
Upon the one who fain had loosed the curse
On others.—An my counsel be worth aught,
Then have a care thy spells do not revert
Upon thyself, nor yet mine own poor hulk
O' fearsomeness!

CRESTILLOMEEM.

Ha! ha!   No vaguest need
Of apprehension there!—While Krung remains—

[*She abruptly pauses—startled first, then listening curiously and with awed interest. Voice of exquisite melodiousness and fervor heard singing.*]

VOICE.

When kings are kings, and kings are men—
   And the lonesome rain is raining!—
O who shall rule from the red throne then,

And who shall covet the sceptre when—
>   When the winds are all complaining?

When men are men, and men are kings—
>   And the lonesome rain is raining!—
O who shall list as the minstrel sings
Of the crown's fiat, or the signet-ring's,
>   When the winds are all complaining?

CRESTILLOMEEM.

Whence flows such sweetness, and what voice is that?

JUCKLET.

The voice of Spraivoll, an mine ears be whet
And honéd o' late honeyéd memories
Behaunting the deserted purlieus of
The court.

CRESTILLOMEEM.

>   And who is Spraivoll, and what song
Is that besung so blinding exquisite
Of cadenced mystery?

THE FLYING ISLANDS OF THE NIGHT

Jucklet.

     Spraivoll—O Queen,—
Spraivoll The Tune-Fool is she fitly named
By those who meet her ere the day long wanes
And naught but janiteering sparsely frets
The cushioned silences and stagnant dusts
Indifferently resuscitated by
The drowsy varlets in mock servitude
Of so refurbishing the royal halls:
She cometh, alien, from Wunkland—so
Hath she deposed to divers questioners
Who have been smitten of her voice—as rich
In melody as she is poor in mind.
She hath been roosting, pitied of the hinds
And scullions, round about the palace here
For half a node.

Crestillomeem.

    And pray, where is she perched—
This wild-bird woman with her wondrous throat?

THE FLYING ISLANDS OF THE NIGHT

JUCKLET.

Under some dingy cornice, like enough—
Though *wild-bird* she is not, being plumèd in,
Not feathers, but one fustioned stole—the like
Of which so shameth her fair face one needs
Must swear some lusty oaths, but that they shape
Themselves full gentlewise in mildest prayer:—
Not *wild-bird;*—nay, nor *woman*—though, in truth,
She ith a licensed idiot, and drifts
About, as restless and as useless, too,
As any lazy breeze in summer-time.
I'll call her forth to greet your Majesty.
Ho! Spraivoll! Ho! my twittering birdster, flit
Thou hither.

[*Enter* SPRAIVOLL—*from behind group of statuary—
singing.*]

SPRAIVOLL.

Ting-aling! Ling-ting! Tingle-tee!
The moon spins round and round for me!

Wind it up with a golden key.
Ting-aling! Ling-ting! Tingle-tee!

CRESTILLOMEEM.

Who art thou, and what the strange
Elusive beauty and intent of thy
Sweet song? What singest thou, vague, mystic-bird—
What doth the Tune-Fool sing? Ay, sing me what.

SPRAIVOLL. [*Singing.*]

What sings the breene on the wertling-vine,
   And the tweck on the bamner-stem?
Their song, to me, is the same as mine,
   As mine is the same to them—to them—
   As mine is the same to them.

In star-starved glooms where the plustre looms
   With its slender boughs above,
Their song sprays down with the fragrant blooms,—
   And the song they sing is love—is love—
   And the song they sing is love.

THE FLYING ISLANDS OF THE NIGHT

JUCKLET.

Your Majesty may be surprised somewhat,
But Spraivoll cannot talk,—her only mode
Of speech is melody; and thou might'st put
The dowered fool a thousand queries, and,
In like return, receive a thousand songs,
All set to differing tunes—as full of naught
As space is full of emptiness.

CRESTILLOMEEM.

A fool?—
And with a gift so all-divine!—A fool?

JUCKLET.

Ay, warranted!—The Flying Islands all
Might flock in mighty counsel—moult, and shake
Their loosened feathers, and sort every tuft,
Nor ever most minutely quarry there
One other Spraivoll, itching with her voice
Such favored spot of cuticle as she
Alone selects here in our blissful realm.

CRESTILLOMEEM.

Out, jester, on thy cumbrous wordiness!
Come hither, Tune-Fool, and be not afraid,
For I like fools so well I married one:
And since thou art a *Queen* of fools, and he
A *King*, why, I've a mind to bring ye two
Together in some wise. Canst use thy song
All times in such entrancing spirit one
Who lists must so needs list, e'en though the song
Go on unceasingly indefinite?

SPRAIVOLL. [*Singing.*]

> If one should ask me for a song,
>   Then I should answer, and my tongue
> Would twitter, trill and troll along
>   Until the song were done.
>
> Or should one ask me for my tongue,
>   And I should answer with a song,
> I'd trill it till the song were sung,
>   And troll it all along.

CRESTILLOMEEM.

Thou art indeed a fool, and one, I think,
To serve my present purposes. Give ear.—
And Jucklet, thou, go to the King and bide
His waking: then repeat these words:—"*The Queen
Impatiently awaits his Majesty,
And craves his presence in the Tower of Stars,
That she may there express full tenderly
Her great solicitude.*" And *then*, end thus,—
"*So much she bade, and drooped her glowing face
Deep in the showerings of her golden hair,
And with a flashing gesture of her arm
Turned all the moonlight pallid, saying, 'Haste!'*"

JUCKLET.

And would it not be well to hang a pearl
Or twain upon thy silken lashes?

CRESTILLOMEEM.

                Go!

JUCKLET. [*Exit, singing.*]

This lovely husband's loyal breast
Heaved only as she might suggest,—
To every whimsy she expressed
He proudly bowed and acquiesced.
    He plotted with her, blithe and gay—
    In no flirtation said her nay,—
    He even took her to the play,
    Excused himself and came away.

CRESTILLOMEEM. [*To Spraivoll.*]

Now, Tune-Fool, *junior*, let me theme *thee* for
A song:—An Empress once, with angel in
Her face and devil in her heart, had wish
To breed confusion to her sovereign lord,
And work the downfall of his haughty son—
The issue of a former marriage—who
Bellowsed her hatred to the whitest heat,
For that her own son, by a former lord,
Was born a hideous dwarf, and reared aside

THE FLYING ISLANDS OF THE NIGHT

From the sire's knowing or his princely own—
That *none*, in sooth, might ever chance to guess
The hapless mother of the hapless child.
The Fiends that scar her thus, protect her still
With outward beauty of both face and form.—
It so is written, and so must remain
Till magic greater than their own is found
To hurl against her. So is she secure
And proof above all fear. Now, listen well!—
Her present lord is haunted with a dream,
That he is soon to pass, and so prepares
(*All havoc hath been wrangled with the drugs!*)
The Throne for the ascension of the son,
His cursèd heir, who still doth baffle all
Her arts against him, e'en as though he were
Protected by a skill beyond her own.
Soh! she, the Queen, doth rule the King in all
Save this affectionate perversity
Of favor for the son whom he would raise
To his own place.—And but for this the King
Long since had tasted death and kissed his fate
As one might kiss a bride! But so his Queen

Must needs withhold, not deal, the final blow,
She yet doth bind him, spelled, still trusting her;
And, by her craft and wanton flatteries,
Doth sway his love to every purpose but
The one most coveted.—And for this end
She would make use of thee;—and if thou dost
Her will, as her good pleasure shall direct,
Why, thou shalt sing at court, in silken tire,
Thy brow bound with wild diamonds, and thy hair
Sown with such gems as laugh hysteric lights
From glittering quespar, guenk and plennocynth,—
Ay, even panoplied as might the fair
Form of a very princess be, thy voice
Shall woo the echoes of the listening Throne.

  Spraivoll. [*Crooning abstractedly.*]

And O' shall one—high brother of the air,
In deeps of space—shall he have dream as fair?—
And shall that dream be this?—In some strange place
Of long-lost lands he finds her waiting face—
Comes marvelling upon it, unaware,
Set moonwise in the midnight of her hair,

And is behaunted with old nights of May,
So his glad lips do purl a roundelay
Purloinèd from the echo-triller's beak,
Seen keenly notching at some star's blanch cheek
With its ecstatic twitterings, through dusk
And sheen of dewy boughs of bloom and musk.
For him, Love, light again the eyes of her
That show nor tears nor laughter nor surprise—
For him undim their glamour and the blur
Of dreams drawn from the depths of deepest skies.
He doth not know if any lily blows
As fair of feature, nor of any rose.

CRESTILLOMEEM. [*Aside.*]

O this weird woman! she doth drug mine ears
With her uncanny sumptuousness of song!
[*To Spraivoll.*]   Nay, nay! Give o'er thy tuneful
    maunderings
And mark me further, Tune-Fool—ay, and well:—
At present doth the King lie in a sleep
Drug-wrought and deep as death—the after-phase

Of an unconscious state, in which each act
Of his throughout his waking hours is so
Rehearsed, in manner, motion, deed and word,
Her spies (the Queen's) that watch him, serving there
As guardians o'er his royal slumbers, may
Inform her of her lord's most secret thought.
And lo, her plans have ripened even now
Till, *should he come upon his Throne to-night,*
Where eagerly his counsellors will bide
His coming,—she, the Queen, hath reason to
Suspect her long-designèd purposes
May fall in jeopardy;—but if he *fail,*
Through *any* means, to lend his presence there,—
Then, by a wheedled mandate, *is his Queen*
Empowered with all Sovereignty to reign
And work the royal purposes instead.
Therefore, the Queen hath set an interview—
A conference to be holden with the King,
Which is ordained to fall on noon to-night,
Twelve star-twirls ere the nick the Throne convenes.—
And with her thou shalt go, and bide in wait
Until she signal thee to sing; and then

Shalt thou so work upon his mellow mood
With that un-Spirkly magic of thy voice—
So all bedaze his waking thought with dreams,—
The Queen may, all unnoticed, slip away,
And leave thee singing to a throneless King.

SPRAIVOLL. [*Singing.*]

And who shall sing for the haughty son
   While the good King droops his head?—
And will he dream, when the song is done,
   That a princess fair lies dead?

CRESTILLOMEEM.

The haughty son hath found *his* "Song"—*sweet curse!*—
And may she sing his everlasting dirge!
She comes from that near-floating land of thine,
Naming herself a princess of that realm
So strangely peopled we would fain evade
All mergence, and remain as strange to them
As they to us. No less this Dwainie hath
Most sinuously writhed and lithed her way

Into court-favor here—hath glidden past
The King's encharmèd sight and sleeked herself
Within the very altars of his house—
His line—his blood—his very life:—*AMPHINE!*
Not any Spirkland gentlemaiden might
Aspire so high as *she* hath dared to dare!—
For she, with her fair skin and finer ways,
And beauty second only to the Queen's,
Hath caught the Prince betwixt her mellow palms
And stroked him flutterless. Didst ever thou
In thy land hear of *Dwainie of the Wunks?*

SPRAIVOLL. [*Singing.*]

Ay, Dwainie!—My Dwainie!
    The lurloo ever sings,
A tremor in his flossy crest
    And in his glossy wings.
And Dwainie!—My Dwainie!
    The winno-welvers call;—
But Dwainie hides in Spirkland
    And answers not at all.

The teeper twitters Dwainie!—
>   The tcheucker on his spray
Teeters up and down the wind
>   And will not fly away:
And Dwainie!—My Dwainie!
>   The drowsy oovers drawl;—
But Dwainie hides in Spirkland
>   And answers not at all.

O Dwainie!—My Dwainie!
>   The breezes hold their breath—
The stars are pale as blossoms,
>   And the night as still as death:
And Dwainie!—My Dwainie!
>   The fainting echoes fall;—
But Dwainie hides in Spirkland
>   And answers not at all.

CRESTILLOMEEM.

A melody ecstatic! and—thy words,
Although so meaningless, seem something more—
A vague and shadowy something, eerie-like,

That maketh one to shiver over-chilled
With curious, creeping sweetnesses of pain
And catching breaths that flutter tremulous
With sighs that dry the throat out icily.—
But save thy music! Come! that I may make
Thee ready for thy royal auditor. [*Exeunt.*]

END ACT I.

ACT II.

SCENE I. *A garden of* KRUNG'S *Palace, screened from the moon with netted glenk-vines and blooming zhoomer-boughs, all glimmeringly lighted with star-flakes. An arbor, near which is a table spread with a repast—two seats, drawn either side. A playing fountain, at marge of which* AMPHINE *sits thrumming a trentoraine.*

AMPHINE. [*Improvising.*]

Ah, help me! but her face and brow
Are lovelier than lilies are
Beneath the light of moon and star
That smile as they are smiling now—
White lilies in a pallid swoon
Of sweetest white beneath the moon—

White lilies in a flood of bright
Pure lucidness of liquid light
Cascading down some plenilune
When all the azure overhead
Blooms like a dazzling daisy-bed.—
So luminous her face and brow,
The lustre of their glory, shed
In memory, even, blinds me now.

[*Plaintively addressing instrument.*]

O warbling strand of silver, where, O where
Hast thou unravelled that sweet voice of thine
And left its silken murmurs quavering
In limp thrills of delight? O golden wire,
Where hast thou spilled thy precious twinkerings?—
What thirsty ear hath drained thy melody,
And left me but a wild, delirious drop
To tincture all my soul with vain desire?

[*Improvising.*]

Her face—her brow—her hair unfurled!—
And O the oval chin below,
Carved, like a cunning cameo,

With one exquisite dimple, swirled
With swimming shine and shade, and whirled
The daintiest vortex poets know—
The sweetest whirlpool ever twirled
By Cupid's finger-tip,—and so,
The deadliest maelstrom in the world.

[*Pauses.—Enter* DWAINIE, *behind, in upper bower, unperceived.*]

AMPHINE. [*Again addressing instrument.*]

O Trentoraine! how like an emptièd vase
Thou art—whose clustering blooms of song have
    drooped
And faded, one by one, and fallen away
And left to me but dry and tuneless stems
And crisp and withered tendrils of a voice
Whose thrilling tone, now like a throttled sound,
Lies stifled, faint, and gasping all in vain
For utterance.

[*Again improvising.*]

And O mad wars of blinding blurs
And flashings of lance-blades of light,

Whet glitteringly athwart the sight
That dares confront those eyes of hers!
Let any dewdrop soak the hue
Of any violet through and through,
And then be colorless and dull,
Compared with eyes so beautiful!
I swear ye that her eyes be bright
As noonday, yet as dark as night—
As bright as be the burnished bars
Of rainbows set in sunny skies,
And yet as deep and dark, her eyes,
And lustrous black as blown-out stars.

[*Pauses*—Dwainie *still unperceived, radiantly smiling and wafting kisses down from trellis-window above.*]

Amphine. [*Again to instrument.*]

O empty husk of song!
If deep within my heart the music thou
Hast stored away might find an issuance,
A fount of limpid laughter would leap up
And gurgle from my lips, and all the winds

Would revel with it, riotous with joy;
And Dwainie, in her beauty, would lean o'er
The battlements of night, and, like the moon,
The glory of her face would light the world—
For I would sing of love.

DWAINIE.

              And she would hear,—
And, reaching overhead among the stars,
Would scatter them like daisies at thy feet.

AMPHINE.

O voice, where art thou floating on the air?—
O Seraph-soul, where art thou hovering?

DWAINIE.

I hover in the zephyr of thy sighs,
And tremble lest thy love for me shall fail
To buoy me thus forever on the breath
Of such a dream as Heaven envies.

AMPHINE.

              Ah!

THE FLYING ISLANDS OF THE NIGHT

[*Turning, discovers* DWAINIE—*she feigning, still, invisibility, while he, with lifted eyes and wistful gaze, preludes with instrument—then sings.*]

Linger, my Dwainie! Dwainie, lily-fair,
Stay yet thy step upon the casement-stair—
Poised be thy slipper-tip as is the tine
Of some still star.—Ah, Dwainie—Dwainie mine,
    Yet linger—linger there!

Thy face, O Dwainie, lily-pure and fair,
Gleams i' the dusk, as in thy dusky hair
The moony zhoomer glimmers, or the shine
Of thy swift smile.—Ah, Dwainie—Dwainie mine,
    Yet linger—linger there!

With lifted wrist, whereround the laughing air
Hath blown a mist of lawn and clasped it there,
Waft finger-thipt adieus that spray the wine
Of thy waste kisses to'rd me, Dwainie mine—
    Yet linger—linger there!

What unloosed splendor is there may compare
With thy hand's unfurled glory, anywhere?

THE FLYING ISLANDS OF THE NIGHT

What glint of dazzling dew or jewel fine
May mate thine eyes?—Ah, Dwainie—Dwainie mine!
    Yet linger—linger there!

My soul confronts thee: On thy brow and hair
It lays its tenderness like palms of prayer—
It touches sacredly those lips of thine
And swoons across thy spirit, Dwainie mine,
    The while thou lingerest there.

[*Drops trentoraine, and, with open arms, gazes yearningly on* DWAINIE.]

DWAINIE. [*Raptly.*]

Thy words do wing my being dovewise!

AMPHINE.

Then,
Thou lovest!—O my homing dove, veer down
And nestle in the warm home of my breast!
So empty are mine arms, so full my heart,
The one must hold thee, or the other burst.

DWAINIE. [*Throwing herself in his embrace.*]

Æo's own hand methinks hath flung me here:
O hold me that He may not pluck me back!

AMPHINE.

So closely will I hold thee that not e'en
The hand of death shall separate us.

DWAINIE.

So
May sweet death find us, then, that, woven thus
In the corolla of a ripe caress,
We may drop lightly, like twin plustre-buds,
On Heaven's star-strewn lawn.

AMPHINE.

So do I pray.
But tell me, tender heart, an thou dost love,
Where hast thou loitered for so long?—for thou
Didst promise tryst here with me earlier by
Some several layodemes which I have told
Full chafingly against my finger-tips

Till the full complement, save three, are ranged
Thy pitiless accusers, claiming, each,
So many as their joinèd number be
Shalt thou so many times lift up thy lips
For mine's most lingering forgiveness.
So, save thee, O my Sweet! and rest thee, I
Have ordered merl and viands to be brought
For our refreshment here, where, thus alone,
I may sip words with thee as well as wine.
Why hast thou kept me so athirst?—Why, I
Am jealous of the flattered solitudes
In which thou walkest. [*They sit at table.*]

DWAINIE.

Nay, I will not tell,
Since, an I yielded, countless questions, like
In idlest worth, would waste our interview
In speculations vain.—Let this suffice:—
I stayed to talk with one whom, long ago,
I met and knew, and grew to love, forsooth,
In dreamy Wunkland.—Talked of mellow nights,
And long, long hours of golden olden times

When girlish happiness locked hands with me
And we went spinning round, with naked feet
In swaths of bruisèd roses ankle-deep;
When laughter rang unsilenced, unrebuked,
And prayers went unremembered, oozing clean
From the drowsed memory, as from the eyes
The pure, sweet mother-face that bent above
Glimmered and wavered, blurred, bent closer still
A timeless instant, like a shadowy flame,
Then flickered tremulously o'er the brow
And went out in a kiss.

         AMPHINE. [*Kissing her.*]

                Not like to *this!*
O blessèd lips whose kiss alone may be
Sweeter than their sweet speech! Speak on, and say
Of what else talked thou and thy friend?

            DWAINIE.

                    We talked
Of all the past, ah me! and all the friends
That now await my coming. And we talked

THE FLYING ISLANDS OF THE NIGHT

Of O so many things—so many things—
That I but blend them all with dreams of when,
With thy warm hand clasped close in this of mine,
We cross the floating bridge that soon again
Will span the all-unfathomable gulfs
Of nether air betwixt this isle of strife
And my most glorious realm of changeless peace,
Where summer night reigns ever and the moon
Hangs ever ripe and lush with radiance
Above a land where roses float on wings
And fan their fragrance out so lavishly
That Heaven hath hint of it, and oft therefrom
Sends down to us across the odorous seas
Strange argosies of interchanging bud
And blossom, spice and balm.—Sweet—sweet
Beyond all art and wit of uttering.

Amphine.

O Empress of my listening Soul, speak on,
And tell me all of that rare land of thine!—
For even though I reigned a peerless king
Within mine own, methinks I could fling down

My sceptre, signet, crown and royal might,
And so fare down the thornèd path of life
If at its dwindling end my feet might touch
Upon the shores of such a land as thou
Dost paint for me—*thy* realm! Tell on of it—
And tell me if thy sister-woman there
Is like to thee—Yet nay! for an thou didst,
These eyes would lose all speech of sight
And call not back to thine their utter love.
But tell me of thy brothers.—Are they great,
And can they grapple Æo's arguments
Beyond our skill? or wrest a purpose from
The pink side of the moon at Darsten-tide?
Or cipher out the problem of blind stars,
That ever still do safely grope their way
Among the thronging constellations?

DWAINIE.

Ay!
Ay, they have leaped all earthland barriers
In mine own isle of wisdom-working Wunks:—
'Twas Wunkland's son that voyaged round the moon

THE FLYING ISLANDS OF THE NIGHT

And moored his bark within the molten bays
Of bubbling silver: And 'twas Wunkland's son
That talked with Mars—unbuckled Saturn's belt
And tightened it in squeezure of such facts
Therefrom as even *he* dare not disclose
In full till all his followers, as himself,
Have grown them wings, and gat them beaks and
    claws,
With plumage all bescienced to withstand
All tensest flames—glaze-throated, too, and lung'd
To swallow fiercest-spurted jets and cores
Of embered and unquenchable white heat:
'Twas Wunkland's son that alchemized the dews
And bred all colored grasses that he wist—
Divorced the airs and mists and caught the trick
Of azure-tinting earth as well as sky:
'Twas Wunkland's son that bent the rainbow straight
And walked it like a street, and so returned
To tell us it was made of hammered shine,
Inlaid with strips of selvage from the sun
And burnished with the rust of rotten stars:
'Twas Wunkland's son that comprehended first

All grosser things, and took our worlds apart
And oiled their works with theories that clicked
In glib articulation with the pulse
And palpitation of the systemed facts.—
And, circling ever round the farthest reach
Of the remotest welkin of all truths,
We stint not our investigations to
Our worlds only, but query still beyond.—
For now our goolores say, below these isles
A million million miles, are *other* worlds—
Not like to ours, but *round*, as bubbles are,
And, like them, ever reeling on through space,
And anchorless through all eternity;—
Not like to ours, for our isles, as they note,
Are living things that fly about at night,
And soar above and cling, throughout the day,
Like bats, beneath the bent sills of the skies:
And I myself have heard, at dawn of moon,
A liquid music filtered through my dreams,
As though 'twere myriads of sweet voices, pent
In some o'erhanging realm, had spilled themselves
In streams of melody that trickled through

THE FLYING ISLANDS OF THE NIGHT

The chinks and crannies of a crystal pave,
Until the wasted juice of harmony,
Slow-leaking o'er my senses, laved my soul
In ecstasy divine: And afferhaiks,
Who scour our coasts on missions for the King,
Declare our island's shape is like the zhibb's
When lolling in a trance upon the air
With open wings upslant and motionless.
O such a land it is—so all complete
In all wise habitants, and knowledge, lore,
Arts, sciences, perfected government
And kingly wisdom, worth and majesty—
And *Art*—ineffably above all else:—
The art of the *Romancer*,—fabulous
Beyond the miracles of strangest fact;
The art of *Poesy*,—the sanest soul
Is made mad with its uttering; the art
Of *Music*,—words may not e'en whimper what
The jewel-sounds of song yield to the sense;
And, last,—the art of *Knowing what to Know*,
And how to zoon straight to'rd it like a bee,
Draining or song or poem as it brims

And over-runs with raciest spirit-dew.—
And, *after*,—chaos all to sense like thine,
Till there, translated, thou shalt know as I. . . .
So furnished forth in all things lovable
Is my Land-Wondrous—ay, and thine to be,—
O Amphine, love of mine, it lacks but thy
Sweet presence to make it a paradise!

    [*Takes up trentoraine.*]

And shall I tell thee of the home that waits
For thy glad coming, Amphine?—Listen, then!

Chant-Recitative.

A palace veiled in a glimmering dusk;
    Warm breaths of a tropic air,
Drugged with the odorous marzhoo's musk
    And the sumptuous cyncotwaire—
Where the trembling hands of the lilwing's leaves
    The winds caress and fawn,
While the dreamy starlight idly weaves
    Designs for the damask lawn.

Densed in the depths of a dim eclipse
    Of palms, in a flowery space,

THE FLYING ISLANDS OF THE NIGHT

A fountain leaps from the marble lips
   Of a girl, with a golden vase
Held atip on a curving wrist,
   Drinking the drops that glance
Laughingly in the glittering mist
   Of her crystal utterance.

Archways looped o'er blooming walks
   That lead through gleaming halls;
And balconies where the word-bird talks
   To the tittering waterfalls:
And casements, gauzed with the filmy sheen
   Of a lace that sifts the sight
Through a ghost of bloom on the haunted screen
   That drips with the dews of light.

Weird, pale shapes of sculptured stone,—
   With marble nymphs agaze
Ever in fonts of amber, sown
   With seeds of gold and sprays
Of emerald mosses, ever drowned,
   Where glimpses of shell and gem

THE FLYING ISLANDS OF THE NIGHT

Peer from the depths, as round and round
    The nautilus nods at them.

Faces blurred in a mazy dance,
    With a music, wild and sweet,
Spinning the threads of the mad romance
    That tangles the waltzers' feet:
Twining arms, and warm, swift thrills
    That pulse to the melody,
Till the soul of the dancer dips and fills
    In the wells of ecstasy.

Eyes that melt in a quivering ore
    Of love, and the molten kiss
Jetted forth of the hearts that pour
    Their blood in the moulds of bliss.—
Till, worn to a languor slumber-deep,
    The soul of the dreamer lifts
A silken sail on the gulfs of sleep,
    And into the darkness drifts.

[*The instrument falls from her hands*—AMPHINE, *in stress of passionate delight, embraces her.*]

AMPHINE.

Thou art not all of earth, O angel one!
Nor do I far miswonder me an thou
Hast peered above the very walls of Heaven!
What hast thou seen there?—Didst on Æo bask
Thine eyes and clothe Him with new splendorings?
And strove He to fling back as bright a smile
As thine, the while He beckoned thee within?
And, tell me, didst thou meet an angel there
A-linger at the gates, nor entering
Till I, her brother, joined her?

DWAINIE.

Why, hast thou
A sister dead?—Truth, I have heard of one
Long lost to thee—not dead?

AMPHINE.

Of her I speak,--
And dead, although we know not certainly,
We moan us ever it must needs be death

Only could hold her from us such long term
Of changeless yearning for her glad return.
She strayed away from us long, long ago.—
O and our memories!—Her wondering eyes
That seemed as though they ever looked on things
We might not see—as haply so they did,—
For she went from us, all so suddenly—
So strangely vanished, leaving never trace
Of her outgoing, that I ofttimes think
Her rapt eyes fell along some certain path
Of special glory paven for her feet,
And fashioned of Æo's supreme desire
That she might bend her steps therein and so
Reach Him again, unseen of our mere eyes.
My sweet, sweet sister!—lost to brother—sire—
And, to *her* heart, one dearer than all else,—
Her *lover*—lost indeed!

DWAINIE.

Nay, do not grieve
Thee thus, O loving heart! Thy sister yet
May come to thee in some glad way the Fates

THE FLYING ISLANDS OF THE NIGHT

Are fashioning the while thy tear-drops fall!
So calm thee, while I speak of thine own self.—
For I have listened to a whistling bird
That pipes of waiting danger.   Didst thou note
No strange behavior of thy sire of late?

AMPHINE.

Ay, he is silent, and he walks as one
In some fixed melancholy, or as one
Half waking.—Even his worshipped books seem now
But things on shelves.

DWAINIE.

            And doth he counsel not
With thee in any wise pertaining to
His ailings, or of matters looking toward
His future purposes or his intents
Regarding thine own future fortunings
And his desires and interests therein?
What bearing hath he shown of late toward thee
By which thou might'st beframe some estimate
Of his mind's placid flow or turbulent?

And hath he not so spoken thee at times
Thou hast been 'wildered of his words, or grieved
Of his strange manner?

AMPHINE.

Once he stayed me on
The palace-stair and whispered, "Lo, my son,
Thy young reign draweth nigh—prepare!"—So passed
And vanished as a wraith, so wan he was!

DWAINIE.

And didst thou never reason on this thing,
Nor ask thyself what dims thy father's eye
And makes a brooding shadow of his form?

AMPHINE.

Why, there's a household rumor that he dreams
Death fareth ever at his side, and soon
Shall signal him away.—But *Jucklet* saith
Crestillomeem hath said *the leeches* say

There is no cause for serious concern;
And thus am I assured 'tis nothing more
Than childish fancy of mine aging sire,—
And so, as now, I laugh, full reverently,
And marvel, as I mark his shuffling gait,
And his bestrangered air and murmurous lips,
As by he glideth to and fro, ha! ha!
Ho! ho!—I laugh me many, many times—
Mind, thou, 'tis *reverently* I laugh—ha! ha!—
And wonder, as he glideth ghostly-wise,
If ever *I* shall waver as I walk,
And stumble o'er my beard, and knit my brows,
And o'er the dull mosaics of the pave
Play chequers with mine eyes! Ha! ha!

DWAINIE. [*Aside.*]

How dare—

How dare I tell him? Yet I must—I must!

AMPHINE.

Why, art *thou*, too, grown childish, that thou canst
Find thee waste pleasure talking to thyself

And staring frowningly with eyes whose smiles
I need so much?

DWAINIE.

           Nay, rather say, their tears,
Poor thoughtless Prince! [*Aside.*] (My magic even
    now
Forecasts his kingly sire's near happening
Of nameless hurt and ache and awful stress
Of agony supreme, when he shall stare
The stark truth in the face!)

AMPHINE.

                  What meanest thou?

DWAINIE.

What mean I but thy welfare? Why, I mean,
One hour agone, the Queen, thy mother—

AMPHINE.

                      Nay,
Say only "Queen"!

THE FLYING ISLANDS OF THE NIGHT

DWAINIE.

—The Queen, one hour agone—
As so I learned from source I need not say—
Sent message craving audience with the King
At noon to-night, within the Tower of Stars.—
Thou knowest, only brief space following
The time of her pent session thereso set
In secret with the King alone, *the Throne
Is set, too, to convene; and that the King
Hath lent his seal unto a mandate that,
Should he withhold his presence there, the Queen
Shall be empowered to preside—to reign—
Solely endowed to work the royal will
In lieu of the good King.* Now, therefore, I
Have been advised that she, the Queen, by craft
Connives to hold him absent purposely,
That she may claim the vacancy—for what
Covert design I know not, but I know
It augurs peril to ye both, as to
The Throne's own perpetuity. [*Aside.*] (Again
My magic gives me vision terrible:—

69

The Sorceress' legions balk mine own.—The King
Still hers, yet wavering. O save the King,
Thou Æo!—Render him to us!)

Amphine.

I feel
Thou speakest truth: and yet how know'st thou this?

Dwainie.

Ask me not that; my lips are welded close.—
And, *more,*—since I have dared to speak, and thou
To listen,—Jucklet is accessory,
And even now is plotting for thy fall.
But, Passion of my Soul! think not of me,—
For nothing but sheer magic may avail
To work me harm;—but look thou to thyself!
For thou art blameless cause of all the hate
That rankleth in the bosom of the Queen.
So have thine eyes unslumbered ever, that
No step may steal behind thee—for in this
Unlooked-of way thine enemy will come:
This much I know, but for what fell intent
Dare not surmise.—*So look thou, night and day,*

*That none may skulk upon thee in this wise
Of dastardly attack.* [*Aside.*] (Ha! Sorceress!
Thou palest, tossing wild and wantonly
The smothering golden tempest of thy hair.—
What! lying eyes! *ye* dare to utter *tears?*
Help! help! Yield us the King!)

AMPHINE.

And thou, O sweet!
How art thou guarded and what shield is thine
Of safety?

DWAINIE.

Fear not thou for me at all.—
Possessed am I of wondrous sorcery—
The gift of Holy Magi at my birth:—
Mine enemy must *front* me in assault
And must with mummery of speech assail,
And I will know him in first utterance—
And so may thus disarm him, though he be
A giant thrice in vasty form and force.

[*Singing heard.*]

But, list! what wandering minstrel cometh here
In the young night?

VOICE. [*In distance—singing.*]

The drowsy eyes of the stars grow dim;
The wamboo roosts on the rainbow's rim,
  And the moon is a ghost of shine:
The soothing song of the crule is done,
But the song of love is a soother one,
  And the song of love is mine.
  Then, wake! O wake!
  For the sweet song's sake,
    Nor let my heart
    With the morning break!

AMPHINE.

Some serenader. Hist!
What meaneth he so early, and what thus
Within the palace garden-close? Quick; here!
He neareth! Soh! Let us conceal ourselves
And mark his action, wholly unobserved.

[AMPHINE *and* DWAINIE *enter bower.*]

VOICE. [*Drawing nearer.*]

The mist of the morning, chill and gray,
Wraps the night in a shroud of spray;
  The sun is a crimson blot:

THE FLYING ISLANDS OF THE NIGHT

The moon fades fast, and the stars take wing;
The comet's tail is a fleeting thing—
    But the tale of love is not.
  Then, wake! O wake!
  For the sweet song's sake,
    Nor let my heart
  With the morning break!

[*Enter* JUCKLET.]

JUCKLET.

Eex! what a sumptuous darkness is the Night—
How rich and deep and suave and velvety
Its lovely blackness to a soul like mine!
Ah, Night! thou densest of all mysteries—
Thou eeriest of unfathomable delights,
Whose soundless sheer inscrutability
Is fascination's own ethereal self,
Unseen, and yet embodied—palpable,—
An essence, yet a form of stableness
That stays me—weighs me, as a giant palm
Were laid on either shoulder.—Peace! I cease
Even to strive to grope one further pace,
But stand uncovered and with lifted face.

O but a glamour of inward light
Hath smitten the eyes of my soul to-night!
Groping here in the garden-land,
I feel my fancy's outheld hand
Touch the rim of a realm that seems
Like an isle of bloom in a sea of dreams:
I stand mazed, dazed and alone—alone!—
My heart beats on in an undertone,
And I lean and listen long, and long,
And I hold my breath as I hear again
The chords of a long-dead trentoraine
And the wraith of an old love-song.
Low to myself am I whispering:—

> *Glad am I, and the night knows why—*
> *Glad am I that the dream came by*
> *And found me here as of old when I*
>   *Was a ruler and a king.*

DWAINIE. [*To Amphine.*]

What gentle little monster is this **dwarf**—
Surely not Jucklet of the court?

THE FLYING ISLANDS OF THE NIGHT

AMPHINE. [*Ironically.*]

Ay, ay!
But he'll *ungentle* an thy woman's-heart
Yield him but space. Listen: he mouths again.

JUCKLET.

It was an age ago—an age
Turned down in life like a folded page.—
See where the volume falls apart,
And the faded bookmark—'tis my heart,—
Nor mine alone, but another knit
So cunningly in the love of it
That you must look, with a shaking head,
Nor know the quick one from the dead.
Ah! what a broad and sea-like lawn
Is the field of love they bloom upon!—
Waves of its violet-velvet grass
Billowing, with the winds that pass,
And breaking in a snow-white foam
Of lily-crests on the shores of home.
Low to myself am I whispering:—

Glad am I, and the Night knows why—
Glad am I that the dream came by
And found me here as of old when I
  Was a ruler and a king.

[*Abruptly breaking into impassioned vocal burst.*]

Song.

Fold me away in your arms, O Night—
  Night, my Night, with your rich black hair!—
Tumble it down till my yearning sight
And my unkissed lips are hidden quite
  And my heart is havened there,—
    Under that mystical dark despair—
    Under your rich black hair.

Oft have I looked in your eyes, O Night—
  Night, my Night, with your rich black hair!—
Looked in your eyes till my face waned white
And my heart laid hold of a mad delight
  That moaned as I held it there
    Under the deeps of that dark despair—
    Under your rich black hair.

THE FLYING ISLANDS OF THE NIGHT

Just for a kiss of your mouth, O Night—
   Night, my Night, with your rich black hair!—
Lo! will I wait as a dead man might
Wait for the Judgment's dawning light,
   With my lips in a frozen prayer—
     Under this lovable dark despair—
     Under your rich black hair.

[*With swift change to mood of utter gayety.*]

Ho! ho! what will my dainty mistress say
When I shall stand knee-deep in the wet grass
Beneath her lattice, and with upturned eyes
And tongue out-lolling like the clapper of
A bell, outpour her *that?* I wonder now
If she will not put up her finger thus,
And say, "Hist! heart of mine! the angels call
To thee!" Ho! ho! Or will her blushing face
Light up her dim boudoir and, from her glass,
Flare back to her a flame upsprouting from
The hot-cored socket of a soul whose light
She thought long since had guttered out?—Ho! ho!

Or, haply, will she chastely bend above—
A Parian phantomette, with head atip
And twinkling fingers dusting down the dews
That glitter on the tarapyzma-vines
That riot round her casement—gathering
Lush blooms to pelt me with while I below
All winkingly await the fragrant shower?
Ho! ho! how jolly is this thing of love!
But how much richer, rarer, jollier
Than all the loves is this rare love of mine!
Why, my sweet Princess doth not even dream
I *am* her lover,—for, to here confess,
I have a way of wooing all mine own,
And waste scant speech in creamy compliment
And courtesies all gaumed with winy words.—
In sooth, I do not woo at all—I *win!*
How is it now the old duet doth glide
Itself full ripplingly adown the grooves
Of its quaint melody?—And whoso, by
The *bye*, or by the *way*, or *for the nonce*,
Or, eke ye, *peradventure*, ever durst
Render a duet singly but myself?

THE FLYING ISLANDS OF THE NIGHT

[*Singing—with grotesque mimicry of two voices.*]

JUCKLET'S OSTENSIBLE DUET.

How is it you woo?—and now answer me true,—
   How is it you woo and you win?
Why, to answer you true,—the first thing that you do
   Is to simply, my dearest—begin.

But how can I begin to woo or to win
   When I don't know a Win from a Woo?
Why, cover your chin with your fan or your fin,
   And I'll introduce them to you.

But what if it drew from my parents a view
   With my own in no manner akin?
No matter!—your view shall be first of the two,—
   So I hasten to usher them in.

Nay, stay! Shall I grin at the Woo or the Win?
   And what will he do if I *do?*
Why, the Woo will begin with "How pleasant it's been!"
   And the Win with "Delighted with you!"

Then supposing he grew very dear to my view—
   I'm speaking, you know, of the Win?

Why, then, you should do what he wanted you to,—
  And now is the time to begin.

The time to begin? O then usher him in—
  Let him say what he wants me to do.
He is here.—He's a twin of yourself,—I am " Win,"
  And you are, my darling, my " Woo"!

[*Capering and courtesying to feigned audience.*]

That song I call most sensible nonsense;
And if the fair and peerless Dwainie were
But here, with that sweet voice of hers, to take
The part of "Woo," I'd be the happiest "Win"
On this side of futurity!   Ho! ho!

DWAINIE.   [*Aside to* AMPHINE.]

What means he?

AMPHINE.

Why, he means that throatless head
Of his needs further chucking down betwixt
His cloven shoulders!
  [*Starting forward—Dwainie detaining him.*]

DWAINIE.

                Nay, thou shalt not stir!
See! now the monster hath discovered our
Repast. Hold! Let us mark him further.

        JUCKLET. [*Archly eying viands.*]

                          What!
A roasted wheffle and a toc-spiced whum,
Tricked with a larvey and a gherghgling's tail!—
And, sprit me! wine enough to swim them in!
Now I should like to put a question to
The *guests;* but as there *are* none, I direct
Mine interrogatory to the host. [*Bowing to vacancy.*]
Am I behind-time?—Then I can but trust
My tardy coming may be overlooked
In my most active effort to regain
A gracious tolerance by service now:—
Directing rapt attention to the fact
That I have brought mine appetite along,

I can but feel, ho! ho! that further words
Would be a waste of speech.
[*Sits at table—pours out wine, drinks and eats voraciously.*]
                          —There was a time
When I was rather backward in my ways
In courtly company (as though, forsooth,
I felt not, from my very birth, the swish
Of royal blood along my veins, though bred
Amongst the treacled scullions and the thralls
I shot from, like a cork, in youthful years,
Into court-favor by my wit's sheer stress
Of fomentation.—*Pah! the stench o' toil!*)
Ay, somehow, as I think, I've all outgrown
That coarse, nice age, wherein one makes a meal
Of two estardles and a fork of soup.
Hey! sanaloo! Lest my starved stomach stand
Awe-stricken and aghast, with mouth agape
Before the rich profusion of this feast,
I lubricate it with a glass of merl
And coax it on to more familiar terms
Of fellowship with those delectables.
[*Pours wine and holds up goblet with mock courtliness.*]

THE FLYING ISLANDS OF THE NIGHT

Mine host!—Thou of the viewless presence and
Hush-haunted lip:—Thy most imperial,
Ethereal, and immaterial health!
Live till the sun dries up, and comb thy cares
With star-prongs till the comets fizzle out
And fade away and fail and are no more!
      [*Drains and refills goblet.*]
And, if thou wilt permit me to observe,—
The gleaming shaft of spirit in this wine
Goes whistling to its mark, and full and fair
Zipps to the target-centre of my soul!
Why, now am I the veriest gentleman
That ever buttered woman with a smile,
And let her melt and run and drip and ooze
All over and around a wanton heart!
And if my mistress bent above me now,
In all my hideous deformity,
I think she would look over, as it were,
The hump upon my back, and so forget
The kinks and knuckles of my crooked legs,
In this enchanting smile, she needs must leap,
Love-dazzled, and fall faint and fluttering

Within these yawning, all-devouring arms
Of mine! Ho! ho! And yet Crestillomeem
Would have me blight my dainty Dwainie with
This feather from the Devil's wing!—But I
Am far too full of craft to spoil the eyes
That yet shall pour their love like nectar out
Into mine own,—and I am far too deep
For royal wit to wade my purposes.

DWAINIE. [*To* AMPHINE.]

What can he mean?

AMPHINE. [*Chafing in suppressed frenzy.*]

Ha! to rush forward and
Tear out his tongue and slap it in his face!

DWAINIE. [*To* AMPHINE.]

Nay, nay! Hist what he saith!

JUCKLET.

How big a fool—
How all magnificent an idiot

THE FLYING ISLANDS OF THE NIGHT

Would I be to blight *her*—(my peerless one!—
My very soul's soul!) as Crestillomeem
Doth instigate me to, for *her* hate's sake—
And inward *jealousy*, as well, belike!—
Wouldst have my Dwainie blinded to my charms—
For charms, good sooth, were every several flaw
Of my malformèd outer-self, compared
With that his Handsomeness the Prince Amphine
Shalt change to at a breath of my puff'd cheek,
E'en were it weedy-bearded at the time
With such a stubble as a huntsman well
Might lose his spaniel in! Ho! ho! Ho! ho!
I fear me, O my coy Crestillomeem,
Thine ancient coquetry doth challenge still
Thine own vain admiration overmuch!
I to crush *her?*—when thou, as certainly,
Hast armed me to smite down the only bar
That lies betwixt her love and mine? Ho! ho!
Hey! but the revel I shall riot in
Above the beauteous Prince, instantuously
Made all abhorrent as a reptiled bulk!
Ho! ho! my princely wooer of the fair

Rare lady of mine own superior choice!
Pah! but my very 'maginings of him
Refinèd to that shamèd, sickening shape,
Do so beloathe me of him there be qualms
Expostulating in my forum now!
Ho! what unprincifying properties
Of medication hath her Majesty
Put in my tender charge! Ho! ho! Ho! ho!
Ah, Dwainie! sweetest sweet! what shock to thee?—
I wonder, when she sees the human toad
Squat at her feet and cock his filmy eyes
Upon her and croak love, if she will not
Call me to tweezer him with two long sticks
And toss him from her path.—O ho! Ho! ho!
Hell bend him o'er some blossom quick, that I
May have one brother in the flesh!

[*Nods drowsily.*]

DWAINIE. [*To* AMPHINE.]

Ha! See!
He groweth drunken.—Soh! Bide yet a spell
And I will vex him with my sorcery:

THE FLYING ISLANDS OF THE NIGHT

Then shall we hence,—for lo, the node when all
Our subtlest arts and strategies must needs
Be quickened into acts and swift results.
Now bide thou here, and in mute silence mark
The righteous penalty that hath accrued
Upon that dwarfèd monster.

[*She stands, still in concealment from the dwarf, her tense gaze fixed upon him as though in mute and painful act of incantation.*—JUCKLET *affected drowsily—yawns and mumbles incoherently—stretches, and gradually sinks at full length on the sward.*—DWAINIE *moves forward—*AMPHINE, *following, is about to set foot contemptuously on sleeper's breast, but is caught and held away by* DWAINIE, *who imperiously waves him back, and still, in pantomime, commanding, bids him turn and hide his face—*AMPHINE *obeying as though unable to do otherwise.* DWAINIE *then unbinds her hair, and throwing it all forward covering her face and bending till it trails the ground, she lifts to the knee her dress, and so walks backward in a circle round the sleeping* JUCKLET, *crooning to herself an incoherent* *song. Then pausing, letting fall her gown, and rising to full stature, waves her hands above the sleeper's face, and runs to* AMPHINE, *who turns about and gazes on her with new wonderment.*]

DWAINIE. [*To* AMPHINE.]

Now shalt thou
Look on such scaith as thou hast never dreamed.

[*As she speaks, half averting her face as with melancholy apprehension, chorus of lugubrious voices heard chanting discordantly.*]

VOICES.

When the fat moon smiles,
    And the comets kiss,
        And the elves of Spirkland flit,
The Whanghoo twunkers
    A tune like this,
        And the Nightmares champ the bit.

[*As chorus dies away, a comet, freighted with weird shapes, dips from the night and trails near* JUCKLET'S *sleeping figure, while, with attendant goblin-forms, two* Night-mares, CREECH *and* GRITCHFANG, *alight.— The comet hisses, switches its tail and disappears, while the two goblins hover buzzingly over* JUCKLET, *who starts wide-eyed and stares fixedly at them, with horribly contorted features.*]

CREECH. [*To* GRITCHFANG.]

Buzz!
    Buzz!
        Buzz!
            Buzz!
Flutter your wings like your grandmother does!
Tuck in your chin and wheel over and *whir-r-r*
Like a dickerbug fast in the web of the wuhrr!
Reel out your tongue, and untangle your toes
And rattle your claws o'er the bridge of his nose;
Tickle his ears with your feathers and fuzz,
And keep up a hum like your grandmother does!

[JUCKLET *moans and clutches at air convulsively.*]

AMPHINE. [*Shuddering.*]

Most grewsome sight! See how the poor worm
 writhes!
How must he suffer!

DWAINIE.

Ay, but good is meant—
A far voice sings it so.

GRITCHFANG. [*To* CREECH.]

Let me dive deep in his nostriline caves,
And keep an eye out as to how he behaves:
Fasten him down while I put him to rack—
And don't let him flop from the flat of his back!
[*Shrinks to minute size, while goblin attendants pluck from
 shrubbery a great lily-shaped flower which they invert
 funnel-wise, with small end at sleeper's nostrils, hoist-
 ing* GRITCHFANG *in at top and jostling shape downward
 gradually from sight, and—removing flower,—voice of*

GRITCHFANG *continues gleefully from within sleeper's head.*]

Ho! I have bored through the floor of his brains,
And set them all writhing with torturous pains;
And I shriek out the prayer, as I whistle and whiz,
I may be the nightmare that my grandmother is!

[*Reappears, through reversal of flower-method, assuming former shape, crosses to* CREECH, *and, joining, the twain dance on sleeper's stomach in broken time to duo.*]

Duo.

Whing!

    Whang!

        So our ancestors sang!
And they guzzled hot blood and blew up with a *bang!*—
But they ever tenaciously clung to the rule
To only blow up in the hull of a fool—
To fizz and explode like a cast-iron toad
In the cavernous depths where his victuals were
    stowed—

When chances were ripest and thickest and best
To burst every button-hole out of his vest!

[*They pause, float high above, and fusing together into a great square iron weight, drop heavily on chest of sleeper, who moans piteously.*]

    AMPHINE. [*Hiding his face.*]

     Ah! take me hence!

[DWAINIE *leads him off, looking backward as she goes and waving her hands imploringly to* CREECH *and* GRITCHFANG, *reassuming former shapes, in ecstasies of insane delight.*]

    CREECH. [*To* GRITCHFANG.]

Zipp!
  Zipp!
    Zipp!
      Zipp!
Sting his tongue raw and unravel his lip!
Grope, on the right, down his windpipe, and squeeze
His liver as dry as a petrified wheeze!

[GRITCHFANG—*as before—shrinks and disappears at sleeper's mouth.*]

Throttle his heart till he's black in the face,
And bury it down in some desolate place
Where only remorse in pent agony lives
To dread the advice that your grandmother gives!

[*The sleeper struggles contortedly, while voice of* GRITCHFANG *calls from within.*]

GRITCHFANG.

Ho-ho! I have clambered the rungs of his ribs
And beriddled his lungs into tatters and dribs;
And I turn up the tube of his heart like a hose
And squirt all the blood to the end of his nose!
I stamp on his stomach and caper and prance,
With my tail tossing round like a boomerang-lance!
And thus may success ever crown my intent
To wander the ways that my grandmother went!

[*Reappears, falls hysterically in* CREECH'S *outstretched arms.—Then dance and duo:*]

Duo.

Whing!
 Whung!
  So our ancestors sung!
And they snorted and pawed, and they hissed and they stung,—
Taking special terrific delight in their work
On the fools that they found in the lands of the Spirk.—
And each little grain of their powders of pain
They scraped up and pestled again and again—
Mixed in quadruple doses for gluttons and sots,
Till they strangled their dreams with gung-jibbrious knots!

[*The comet again trails past, upon which the* Nightmares *leap and disappear.* JUCKLET *staggers to his feet and glares frenziedly around—then starts for opposite exit of comet—is there suddenly confronted with fiend-faces in the air, bewhiskered with ragged purplish flames that flare audibly and huskily in abrupt alternating chill gasps and hot welterings of wind. He starts back from them, reels and falls prostrate, grovelling ter-rifiedly in the dust, and chattering, with eerie music accompanying his broken utterance.*]

JUCKLET.

Æo! Æo! Æo!
Thou that dost all things know—
    Waiving all claims of mine to *dare* to pray,
Save that I needs *must:*—Lo,
    What *may* I pray for? Yea,
    I have not *any* way,
An *Thou* gainsayest me a tolerance so.—
    I dare not pray
        Forgiveness—too great
        My vast o'ertoppling weight
    Of sinning; nor can I
    Pray my
Poor soul unscourged to go.—
Frame *Thou* my prayer, Æo!

What may I pray for? Dare
I shape a prayer,

In sooth,
 For any cancelled joy
  Of my mad youth,
   Or any bliss my sin's stress did destroy?
What may I pray for—What?—
That the wild clusters of forget-me-not
  And mignonette
  And violet
Be out of childhood brought,
   And in mine hard heart set
  A-blooming now as then?—
   With all their petals yet
Bediamonded with dews—
Their sweet, sweet scent let loose
  Full sumptuously again!

What *may* I pray, Æo!
 For the poor hutchèd cot
 Where death sate squat
Midst my first memories?—Lo!
My mother's face—(they, whispering, told me
 so)—

That face!—so pinchedly
It blanched up, as they lifted me—
    Its frozen eyelids would
    Not part, nor could
Be ever wetted open with warm tears.
. . . Who hears
The prayers for all dead-mother-sakes, Æo!

Leastwise *one* mercy:—May
I not have leave to pray
All *self* to pass away—
    Forgetful of all needs mine own—
    Neglectful of all creeds;—alone,
Stand fronting Thy high throne and say:
    To Thee,
O Infinite, I pray
    Shield *Thou* mine enemy!

[*Music throughout supplication gradually softens and sweetens into utter gentleness, with scene slow-fading into densest night.*]

END ACT II.

ACT III.

SCENE I. *Court of* KRUNG—*Royal Ministers, Counsellors, etc., in session.* CRESTILLOMEEM, *in full blazonry of regal attire, presiding. She signals a Herald at her left, who steps forward.—Blare of trumpets, greeted with ominous murmurings within, blent with tumult from without.*

HERALD.

Hist, ho! Ay, ay! Ay, ay!—Her Majesty,
The All-Glorious and Ever-Gracious Queen,
Crestillomeem, to her most loyal, leal
And right devoted subjects, greeting sends—
Proclaiming, in the absence of the King,
Her royal presence—

[*Voice of* Herald *fails abruptly—utterly.—A breathless hush falls sudden on the court.—A sense oppressive—ominous—affects the throng. Weird music heard of unseen instruments.*]

HERALD. [*Huskily striving to be heard.*]

Hist, ho! Ay, ay! Ay, ay!—Her Majesty,
The All-Glorious and Ever-Gracious Queen,
Crestillomeem—

[*The* Queen *gasps, and clutches at* Herald, *mutely signing him to silence, her staring eyes fixed on a shadowy figure, mistily developing before her into wraith-like form and likeness of the Tune-Fool,* SPRAIVOLL. *The shape—evidently invisible and voiceless to all senses but the* Queen's—*wavers vaporishly to and fro before her, moaning and crooning in infinitely sweet-sad minor cadences a mystic song.*]

WRAITH-SONG OF SPRAIVOLL.

I will not hear the dying word
Of any friend, nor stroke the wing

Of any little wounded bird.
. . . Love is the deadest thing!

I wist not if I see the smile
Of prince or wight, in court or lane.—
I only know that afterwhile
He will not smile again.

The summer blossom, at my feet,
Swims backward, drowning in the grass.—
I will not stay to name it sweet—
Sink out! and let me pass!

I have no mind to feel the touch
Of gentle hands on brow and hair.—
The lack of this once pained me much,
And so I have a care.

Dead weeds, and husky-rustling leaves
That beat the dead boughs where ye cling,
And old dead nests beneath the eaves—
Love is the deadest thing!

THE FLYING ISLANDS OF THE NIGHT

Ah! once I fared not all alone;
  And once—no matter, rain or snow!—
The stars of summer ever shone—
  Because I loved him so!

With always tremblings in his hands,
  And always blushes unaware,
And always ripples down the strands
  Of his long yellow hair.

I needs must weep a little space,
  Remembering his laughing eyes
And curving lip, and lifted face
  Of rapture and surprise.

O joy is dead in every part,
  And life and hope; and so I sing:
In all the graveyard of my heart
  Love is the deadest thing!

[*With dying away of song, apparition of* SPRAIVOLL *slowly vanishes.* CRESTILLOMEEM *turns dazedly to throng, and with labored effort strives to reassume imperious mien.—Signs for merl and tremulously drains goblet— sinks back in throne with feigned complacency, mutely waving* Herald *to proceed.*]

HERALD. [*Mechanically.*]

Hist, ho! Ay, ay! Ay, ay!—Her Majesty,
The All-Glorious and Ever-Gracious Queen,
Crestillomeem, to her most loyal, leal
And right devoted subjects, greeting sends—
Proclaiming, in the absence of the King,
Her royal presence, as by him empowered
To sit and occupy, maintain and hold,
And therefrom rule the Throne, in sovereign state,
And work the royal will—[*Confusion.*] Hist, ho! Ay,
  ay!
Ay, ay!—And be it known, the King, in view
Of his approaching dissolution—

[*Sensation among* Counsellors, *etc., within, and wild tumult without and cries* "*Long live the* King!" *and* "*Treason!*" "*Intrigue!*" "*Sorcery!*" CRESTILLOMEEM, *in suppressed ire, waving silence, and* Herald *striving to be heard.*]

THE FLYING ISLANDS OF THE NIGHT

HERALD.

Hist, ho! Ay, ay! Ay, ay!—The King, in view
Of his approaching dissolution, hath
Decreed this instrument—this royal scroll
    [*Unrolling and displaying scroll.*]
With royal seal thereunto set by Krung's
Most sacred act and sign—

[*General sensation within, and growing tumult without, with wrangling cries of " Plot !" " Treason !" " Conspiracy!" and " Down with the* Queen!" "*Down with the usurper!*" "*Down with the Sorceress !*"]

CRESTILLOMEEM. [*Wildly.*]

Who dares to cry
"Conspiracy!" Bring me the traitor-knave!

[*Growing confusion without—sound of rioting.—Voice, " Let me be taken! Let me be taken!" Enter* Guards, *dragging* JUCKLET *forward, wild-eyed and hysterical —the* Queen's *gaze fastened on him wonderingly.*]

CRESTILLOMEEM. [*To* Guards.]

Why bring ye Jucklet hither in this wise?

GUARD.

O Queen, 'tis he who cries "Conspiracy!"
And who incites the mob without with cries
Of "Plot!" and "Treason!"

CRESTILLOMEEM. [*Starting.*]

Ha! Can this be true?
I'll not believe it!—Jucklet is my fool,
But not so vast a fool that he would tempt
His gracious Sovereign's ire. [*To* Guards.] Let him be freed!
 [*Then to* JUCKLET, *with mock service.*]
Stand hither, O my Fool!

JUCKLET. [*To* Queen.]

What! I, thy fool?
Ho! ho! *Thy* fool?—ho! ho!—Why, *thou* art *mine!*

[*Confusion—cries of "Strike down the traitor!"* JUCKLET *wrenching himself from grasp of officers.*]

  Back, all of ye! I have not waded hell
  That I should fear your puny enmity!
  Here will I give ye proof of all I say!

[*Presses toward throne, wedging his opposers left and right—*CRESTILLOMEEM *sits as though stricken speechless—pallid, waving him back—*JUCKLET, *fairly fronting her, with folded arms—then to throng continues.*]

  Lo! do I here defy her to lift up
  Her voice and say that Jucklet speaks a lie.

[*At sign of* Queen, *officers, unperceived by Jucklet, close warily behind him.*]

  And, further—I pronounce the document
  That craven Herald there holds in his hand
  A forgery—a trick—and dare the Queen,
  Here in my listening presence, to command
  Its further utterance!

          CRESTILLOMEEM. [*Wildly rising.*]

                Hold, hireling!—Fool!—
  The Queen thou dost in thy mad boasts insult
  Shall utter first thy doom!

[JUCKLET, *seized from behind by* Guards, *is hurled face upward on the dais at her feet, while a minion, with drawn sword pressed close against his breast, stands over him.*]
        —Ere we proceed
With graver matters, let this demon-knave
Be sent back home to hell.
[*With awful stress of ire, form quivering, eyes glittering and features twitched and ashen.*]
         Give *me* the sword,—
The insult hath been mine—so even shall
The vengeance be!

[*As* CRESTILLOMEEM *seizes sword and bends forward to strike,* JUCKLET, *with superhuman effort, frees his hand, and, with a sudden motion and an incoherent muttering, flings object in his assailant's face,*—CRESTILLOMEEM *staggers backward, dropping sword, and, with arms tossed aloft, shrieks, totters and falls prone upon the pave. In confusion following* JUCKLET *mysteriously vanishes; and as the bewildered* Courtiers *lift the fallen* Queen, *a clear, piercing voice of thrilling sweetness is heard singing.*]

THE FLYING ISLANDS OF THE NIGHT

VOICE.

The pride of noon must wither soon—
   The dusk of death must fall;
Yet out of darkest night the moon
   Shall blossom over all!

[*For an instant a dense cloud envelops empty throne—then gradually lifts, discovering therein* KRUNG *sected, in royal panoply and state, with* JUCKLET *in act of presenting sceptre to him.—Blare of trumpets, and chorus of* Courtiers, Ministers, Heralds, *etc.*]

CHORUS.

All hail! Long live the King!

KRUNG. [*To throng, with grave salutation.*]

Through Æo's own great providence, and through
The intervention of an angel whom
I long had deemed forever lost to me,
Once more your favored Sovereign, do I greet
And tender ye my blessing, O most good
And faith-abiding subjects of my realm!

In common, too, with your long-suffering King,
Have *ye* long suffered, blamelessly as he:
Now, therefore, know ye all what, until late,
He knew not of himself, and with him share
The rapturous assurance that is his,—
That, for all time to come, are we restored
To the old glory and most regal pride
And opulence and splendor of our realm.

[*Turning with pained features to the strangely stricken Queen.*]

There have been, as ye needs must know, strange spells
And wicked sorceries at work within
The very dais-boundaries of the Throne.
Lo! then, behold your harrier and mine,
And with me grieve for the self-ruined Queen
Who grovels at my feet, blind, speechless, and
So stricken with a curse herself designed
Should light upon Hope's fairest minister.

[*Motions attendants, who lead away* CRESTILLOMEEM—*the King gazing after her, overmastered with stress of his emotions.—He leans heavily on throne, as though obliv-*

ious to all surroundings, and, shaping into speech his varying thought, as in a trance, speaks as though witless of both utterance and auditor.]

I loved her.—Why? I never knew.—Perhaps
Because her face was fair; perhaps because
Her eyes were blue and wore a weary air;—
Perhaps . . . perhaps because her limpid face
Was eddied with a restless tide, wherein
The dimples found no place to anchor and
Abide: perhaps because her tresses beat
A froth of gold about her throat, and poured
In splendor to the feet that ever seemed
Afloat. Perhaps because of that wild way
Her sudden laughter overleapt propriety;
Or—who will say?—perhaps the way she wept.
Ho! have ye seen the swollen heart of summer
Tempest, o'er the plain, with throbs of thunder
Burst apart and drench the earth with rain? She
Wept like that.—And to recall, with one wild glance
Of memory, our last love-parting—tears
And all. . . . It thrills and maddens me! And yet
My dreams will hold her, flushed from lifted brow

To finger-tips, with passion's ripest kisses
Crushed and mangled on her lips. . . . O woman! while
Your face was fair, and heart was pure, and lips
Were true, and hope as golden as your hair,
I should have strangled you!
[*As* KRUNG, *ceasing to speak, piteously lifts his face,* SPRAI-
 VOLL *all suddenly appears, in space left vacant by the*
 Queen, *and, kneeling, kisses the* King's *hand.—*
 He bends in tenderness, kissing her brow—then lifts
 and seats her at his side. Speaks then to throng.]
      Good Subjects—Lords:
Behold in this sweet woman here my child,
Whom, years agone, the cold, despicable
Crestillomeem—by baleful, wicked arts
And grewsome spells and fearsome witcheries—
Did spirit off to some strange otherland,
Where, happily, a Wunkland Princess found
Her, and undid the spell by sorcery
More potent—ay, *Divine*, since it works naught
But *good*—the gift of Æo, to right wrong.
This magic dower the Wunkland Princess hath
Enlisted in our restoration here,

In secret service, till this joyful hour
Of our complete deliverance.   Even thus.—
Lo, let the peerless Princess now appear!

[*He lifts sceptre, and a gust of melody, divinely beautiful,
    sweeps through the court.— The star above the throne
    loosens and drops slowly downward, bursting like a
    bubble on the sceptre-tip, and, issuing therefrom,*
    AMPHINE *and* DWAINIE, *hand in hand, kneel at the
    feet of* KRUNG, *who bends above them with his blessing,
    while* JUCKLET *capers wildly round the group.*]

JUCKLET.

Ho! ho! but I could shriek for very joy!
And though my recent rival, fair Amphine,
Doth even now bend o'er a blossom, I,
Besprit me! have no lingering desire
To meddle with it, though with but one eye
I slept the while she backward walked around
Me in the garden.

[AMPHINE *dubiously smiles—*JUCKLET *blinks and leers—
    and* DWAINIE *bites her finger.*]

Krung.

              Peace! good Jucklet!   Peace!
For this is not a time for any jest.—
Though the old order of our realm hath been
Restored, and though restored my very life—
Though I have found a daughter,—I have lost
A son—for Dwainie, with her sorcery,
Will, on the morrow, carry him away.
'Tis Æo's largess, as our love is His,
And our abiding trust and gratefulness.

        Curtain.

SPIRK AND WUNK RHYMES

ROUNDS AND CATCHES

TO loll back, in a misty hammock, swung
 From tip to tip of a slim crescent moon
 That gems some royal-purple night of June—
To dream of songs that never have been sung
Since the first stars were stilled and God was young
 And heaven as lonesome as a lonesome tune:
 To lie thus, lost to earth, with lids aswoon;
By curious, cool winds back and forward flung,
 With fluttering hair, blurred eyes, and utter ease
Adrift like lazy blood through every vein;
 And then,—the pulse of unvoiced melodies
Timing the raptured sense to some refrain
 That knows nor words, nor rhymes, nor euphonies,
 Save Fancy's hinted chime of unknown seas.

[NOTE.—Only the musical reader who has tried to whistle the elusive airs of an exquisite music-box can rightly appreciate how futile were a general attempt here accurately to reproduce the music of the Spirks and Wunks: So, but one simplest, all-imperfect *illustration* of it is ventured.—Indeed, the imagination may be better looked to for the just translations of the curious airs of such songs as from time to time follow. So, too, in numberless other respects, must the reader's fancy freely play—even as the writer frankly confesses his own has done,— in such particulars, for instance, as fancying the "ont-l-dawn-bird" of the Flying Islanders is our nightingale; their "trance-bird" our humming-bird; their "echo-bird" our mocking-bird, etc., etc., *ad infinitum*.]

THE LOVELY HUSBAND

Oh a love-ly hus-band he was known, He loved his wife and her a-lone; She reaped the har-vest he had sown; She ate the meat; he picked the bone. With mixed ad-mir-ers ev-ery size, She smiled on each with-

THE LOVELY HUSBAND

out dis-guise; This love-ly hus-band closed his eyes Lest he might take her by sur-prise.

CHORUS.

Trot! Run! Was-n't he a han-dy hub-by? What Fun She could plot and plan! Not One Oth-er such a dan-dy hub-by As this love-ly man!

THE LOVELY HUSBAND

II

He answered at her least command:
He fanned her, if she would be fanned;
He vanished when she willed it.—And
He always coughed behind his hand.
  She held him in such high esteem
  She let him dope her face with
   "Cream,"—
  He'd chink the wrinkles seam-by-seam,
  And call her "lovely as a dream!"

CHORUS

Hot
 Bun!
  Wasn't he a lovey-dovey?

What
 Fun
  She could plot and plan!

Not
 One
  Other such a dovey-lovey
  As this love-ly man!

THE LOVELY HUSBAND

III

Her lightest wishes he foreknew
And fell up-stairs to cater to:
He never failed to back from view,
Nor mispronounced *Don't* ( ) *you* "Doan chu."
> He only sought to fill such space
> As her friends left;—he knew his place:—
> He praised the form she could not lace.—
> He praised her face before her face!

CHORUS

Shot
> *Gun!*
>> *Wasn't he a lovely fellow?*

What
> *Fun*
>> *She could plot and plan!*

Not
> *One*
>> *Lonesome little streak of yellow*
>> *In this love-ly man!*

THE LIGHT OF LOVE

Song

The clouds have deepened o'er the night
   Till, through the dark profound,
The moon is but a stain of light,
   And all the stars are drowned;
And all the stars are drowned, my love,
   And all the skies are drear;
But what care we for light above,
   If light of love is here?

The wind is like a wounded thing
   That beats about the gloom
With baffled breast and drooping wing,
   And wail of deepest doom;
And wail of deepest doom, my love;
   But what have we to fear
From night, or rain, or winds above,
   With love and laughter here?

SONGS TUNELESS

I

HE kisses me! Ah, now, at last,
  He says good-night as it should be,
  His great warm eyes bent yearningly
Above my face—his arms locked fast
  About me, and mine own eyes dim
  With happy tears for love of him.

He kisses me! Last night, beneath
  A swarm of stars, he said I stood
  His one fair form of womanhood,
And springing, shut me in the sheath
  Of a caress that almost hid
  Me from the good his kisses did.

He kisses me! He kisses me!
  This is the sweetest song I know,
  And so I sing it very low

And faint, and O so tenderly
>That, though you listen, none but he
May hear it as he kisses me.

II

"How can I make you love me more?"—
>A thousand times she asks me this,
>Her lips uplifted with the kiss
That I have tasted o'er and o'er,
>Till now I drain it with no sense
>Other than utter indolence.

"How can I make you love me more?"—
>A thousand times her questioning face
>Has nestled in its resting-place
Unanswered, till, though I adore
>This thing of being loved, I doubt
>Not I could get along without.

"How can she make me love her more?"—
>Ah! little woman, if, indeed,
>I might be frank as is the need
Of frankness, I would fall before

Her very feet, and there confess
My love were more if hers were less.

III

Since I am old I have no care
  To babble silly tales of when
  I loved, and lied, as other men
Have done, who boasted here and there,
  They would have died for the fair thing
  They after murdered, marrying.

Since I am old I reason thus—
  No thing survives, of all the past,
  But just regret enough to last
Us till the clods have smothered us;—
  Then, with our dead loves, side by side,
  We may, perhaps, be satisfied.

Since I am old, and strive to blow
  Alive the embers of my youth
  And early loves, I find, in sooth,
An old man's heart may burn so low,
  'Tis better just to calmly sit
  And rake the ashes over it.

OUT OF THE DARK AND THE DEARTH

Ho! but the darkness was densely black!
    And young feet faltered and groped their way,
With never the gleam of a star, alack!
    Nor a moonbeam's lamest ray!—
        Blind of light as the blind of sight.—
        And that was the night—the night!

And out of the blackness, vague and vast,
    And out of the dark and the dearth, behold!—
A great ripe radiance grew at last
    And burst like a bubble of gold,
        Gilding the way that the feet danced on.—
        And that was the dawn—The Dawn!

SPIRK TROLL-DERISIVE

I

THE Crankadox leaned o'er the edge of the moon
  And wistfully gazed on the sea—

                              The sea,—

Where the Gryxabodill madly whistled a tune
  To the air of "Ti-fol-de-ding-dee"—

                              Ding-dee—

  To the air of "Ti-fol-de-ding-dee."
    The quavering shriek
    Of the Fly-up-the-creek
  Was fitfully wafted afar—

                              Afar—

To the Queen of the Wunks as she powdered her cheek

With the pulverized rays of a star—
Ar-rar—
The pulverized rays of a star.

II

The Ghost of the Zhack flitted by in a trance,
And the Squidjum hid under a tub—
A tub—
As he heard the loud hooves of the Hooken advance
With a rub-a-dub—dub-a-dub—dub!
Dub-dub!
With a rub-a-dub—dub-a-dub—dub!
And the Crankadox cried,
As he lay down and died,
"My fate there is none to bewail—
Bewail!"
While the Queen of the Wunks drifted over the tide
With a long piece of crape to her tail
So pale—
A long piece of crape to her tail!

THE ROMAUNT OF KING MORDAMEER

Ho! did ye hear of Mordameer,
    The King of Slumberland!
A lotus-crown upon his brow—
    A poppy in his hand,
And all the elves that people dreams
    To bow at his command.

His throne is wrought of blackest night,
    Enriched with rare designs
Wherein the blazing comet runs
    And writhes and wreaths and twines
About a crescent angel-face
    That ever smiling shines.

The dais is of woven rays
    Of starlight fringed with shade,
And jewelled o'er with gems of dew,

And dyed and interlaid
With every gleaming tint and hue
  Of which the flowers are made.

And when the day has died away
  In darkness o'er the land,
The King bends down his dusky face
  And takes the sleeper's hand,
And lightly o'er his folded eyes
  He waves his magic wand.

And lo! within his princely home,
  Upon his downy bed,
With soft and silken coverlets
  And curtains round him spread,
The rich man rolls in troubled sleep,
  And moans in restless dread:

His eyes are closed, yet Mordameer
  May see their stony stare
As plainly fixed in agony
  As though the orbs were bare
And glaring at the wizard throng
  That fills the empty air:—

THE ROMAUNT OF KING MORDAMEER

A thousand shapes, with phantom japes,
    Dance o'er the sleeper's sight,—
With fingers bony-like and lean,
    And faces pinched and white,
And withered cheeks, and sunken eyes
    With ever-ravening sight.

And such the dreams that Mordameer
    Brings to the child of Pride,—
The worn and wasted forms that he
    Hath stinted and denied—
Of those who filled his coffers up
    And empty-handed died.

And then again he waves his wand:
    And from his lair of straw
The felon, with his fettered limbs,
    Starts up with fear and awe,
And stares with starting eyes upon
    A vision of the law:

A grim procession passes by,
    The while he glares in fear—
With faces, from a wanton's smile

Down to a demon's leer,—
The woman marching at the front,
    The hangman at the rear.

All ways are clear to Mordameer:
    The ocean knows his tread;
His feet are free on land or sea:—
    Above the sailor's head
He hangs a dream of home, and bends
    Above his cottage-bed:

And, nestled in the mother's arms,
    A child, surpassing fair,
In slumber lies, its tiny hands
    Entangled in her hair,
And round its face a smile that moves
    Its lips as though in prayer.

And lo! the good king feasts its eyes
    With fruits from foreign shores,
And pink-lipped shells that ever mock
    The ocean as it roars;
And in the mother's arms he folds
    The form that she adores.

THE ROMAUNT OF KING MORDAMEER

Through all the hovels of the poor
  He steals with noiseless tread,
And presses kisses o'er and o'er
  Where sorrow's tears are shed,
Till old caresses live once more
  That are forever dead.

Above the soldier in his tent
  Are glorious battles fought;
And o'er the prince's velvet couch,
  And o'er the peasant's cot,
And o'er the pallet of disease
  His wondrous spells are wrought.

He bends him o'er the artist's cot,
  And fills his dazzled mind
With airy forms that float about
  Like clouds in summer wind,
O'er landscapes that the angels wrought
  And God Himself designed.

And drifting through the poet's dreams
  The seraph trails her wings,
And fills the chancels of his soul

THE ROMAUNT OF KING MORDAMEER

With heavenly whisperings,
Till, swooning with delight, he hears
The song he never sings.

He walks the wide world's every way,
This monarch grand and grim;
All paths that reach the human heart,
However faint and dim,
He journeys, for the darkest night
Is light as day to him.

And thus the lordly Mordameer
Rules o'er his mystic realm,
With gems from out the star's red core
To light his diadem,
And kings and emperors to kneel
And kiss his garment's hem.

For once, upon a night of dreams,
Adown the aisles of space
I strayed so far that I forgot
Mine own abiding-place,
And wandered into Slumberland,
And met him face to face.

DEATH

Lo, I am dying! And to feel the King
Of Terrors fasten on me, steeps all sense
Of life, and love, and loss, and everything,
In such deep calms of restful indolence,
His keenest fangs of pain are sweet to me
As fusèd kisses of mad lovers' lips
When, flung shut-eyed in spasmed ecstasy,
They feel the world spin past them in eclipse,
And so thank God with ever-tightening lids!
But what I see, the soul of me forbids
All utterance of; and what I hear and feel,
The rattle in my throat could ill reveal
Though it were music to your ears as to
Mine own.—Press closer—closer—I have grown
So great, your puny arms about me thrown

DEATH

Seem powerless to hold me here with you;—
I slip away—I waver—and—I fall—
Christ! What a plunge! Where am I dropping? All
My breath bursts into dust—I cannot cry—
I whirl—I reel and veer up overhead,
And drop flat-faced against—against—the sky—
Soh, bless me! I am dead!

WE ARE NOT ALWAYS GLAD WHEN WE SMILE

We are not always glad when we smile:
  Though we wear a fair face and are gay,
    And the world we deceive
    May not ever believe
  We could laugh in a happier way.—
Yet, down in the deeps of the soul,
  Ofttimes, with our faces aglow,
    There's an ache and a moan
    That we know of alone,
  And as only the hopeless may know.

We are not always glad when we smile,—
  For the heart, in a tempest of pain,
    May live in the guise
    Of a smile in the eyes
  As a rainbow may live in the rain;

WE ARE NOT ALWAYS GLAD WHEN WE SMILE

And the stormiest night of our woe
  May hang out a radiant star
    Whose light in the sky
    Of despair is a lie
  As black as the thunder-clouds are.

We are not always glad when we smile!—
  But the conscience is quick to record,
    All the sorrow and sin
    We are hiding within
  Is plain in the sight of the Lord:
And ever, O ever, till pride
  And evasion shall cease to defile
    The sacred recess
    Of the soul, we confess
  We are not always glad when we smile.

THE WEREWIFE

SHE came to me in a dazzling guise
Of gleaming tresses and glimmering eyes,
With long, limp lashes that drooped and made
For their baleful glances bowers of shade;
And a face so white—so white and sleek
That the roses blooming in either cheek
Flamed and burned with a crimson glow
Redder than ruddiest roses blow—
Redder than blood of the roses know
That Autumn spills in the drifted snow.
And what could my fluttering, moth-winged soul
Do but hover in her control?—
With its little, bewildered bead-eyes fixed
Where the gold and the white and the crimson mixed?
And when the tune of her low laugh went
Up from that ivory instrument

THE WEREWIFE

That you would have called her throat, I swear
The notes built nests in her gilded hair,
And nestled and whistled and twittered there,
And wooed me and won me to my despair.
And thus it was that she lured me on,
Till the latest gasp of my love was gone,
And my soul lay dead, with a loathing face
Turned in vain from her dread embrace,—
For even its poor dead eyes could see
Her sharp teeth sheathed in the flesh of me,
And her dripping lips, as she turned to shake
The red froth off that her greed did make,
As my heart gripped hold of a deathless ache,
And the kiss of her stung like the fang of a snake.

THE RAIN

The rain sounds like a laugh to me—
A low laugh poured out limpidly.

MY very soul smiles as I listen to
  The low, mysterious laughter of the rain,
  Poured musically over heart and brain
Till sodden care, soaked with it through and through,
Sinks; and, with wings wet with it as with dew,
  My spirit flutters up, with every stain
  Rinsed from its plumage, and as white again
As when the old laugh of the rain was new.
  Then laugh on, happy Rain! laugh louder yet!—
Laugh out in torrent-bursts of watery mirth;
  Unlock thy lips of purple cloud, and let
Thy liquid merriment baptize the earth,
  And wash the sad face of the world, and set
  The universe to music dripping-wet!

FOR YOU

For you, I could forget the gay
    Delirium of merriment,
And let my laughter die away
    In endless silence of content.
        I could forget, for your dear sake,
        The utter emptiness and ache
        Of every loss I ever knew.—
        What could I not forget for you?

I could forget the just deserts
    Of mine own sins, and so erase
The tear that burns, the smile that hurts,
    And all that mars and masks my face.
        For your fair sake I could forget
        The bonds of life that chafe and fret,
        Nor care if death were false or true.—
        What could I not forget for you?

FOR YOU

What could I not forget? Ah me!
  One thing I know would still abide
Forever in my memory,
    Though all of love were lost beside—
      I yet would feel how first the wine
      Of your sweet lips made fools of mine
      Until they sung, all drunken through—
      "What could I not forget for you?"

THE STRANGE YOUNG MAN

'Twas a strange young man of the dreamy times
When bards made money, and bankers rhymes;
And drones made honey—and bees made naught;
And the bad sung hymns, and the good-folk fought;
And the merchants lurked in the shade all day
And pitched horseshoes in a listless way!
When the ticket-man at the station knew
If your trunk would go if you checked it through,
And if 2:30 meant half-past two,
And what in-the-name-of-the-land to do
If a man got left when he oughtn't to:
When the cabman wept as he took your fare,
And the street-car driver led in prayer—
And the kuss with the dyed mustache was there

THE STRANGE YOUNG MAN

That rode in town on a "jumper"-sled,
And got whipped twice for the things he said
To fellows that told him his hair was red.
And the strange young man (of which and whom
Our pencil offers to deign presume
To treat of now, in the days like these
When young men dress as they please to please)
Went round in a coat of pale pink-blue,
And a snow-white vest of a crimson hue,
And trousers purple, and gaiters gray—
All cut, as the French or the Dutch would say,—
La—macht nichts aus, oder—décolleté,—
Strange not only in dress, but in
The dimples he wore in cheek and chin—
All nailed over with scraps of tin,
Where he hadn't been shaved as he'd ought o' been;—
And his crape cravat, and the shape of that,
And the ear-tab over his diamond-pin.
And his friends all wondered, and used to say,—
"What a strange young man! Ah me! Hooray!
How sad he seems in his wild delight!
And how tickled indeed when he weeps outright!

THE STRANGE YOUNG MAN

What a comical man when he writhes in pain;
And how grieved he grows when he's glad again!"
And marvelling still to remark new facts,
They said, "How slender and slim he acts!
And isn't it odd for a man to wear
A thumb-stall over his nose, and pare
His finger-nails with a carving-knife,
And talk of prunes to the landlord's wife?
It is patent to us—and, indeed, no doubt,
   Though as safely sealed as an oyster-can,—
Our interest in him must needs leak out,—
   Namely, that he is a strange young man!"

"DREAM"

Because her eyes were far too deep
And holy for a laugh to leap
Across the brink where sorrow tried
To drown within the amber tide;
Because the looks, whose ripples kissed
The trembling lids through tender mist,
Were dazzled with a radiant gleam—
Because of this I called her "Dream."

Because the roses growing wild
About her features when she smiled
Were ever dewed with tears that fell
With tenderness ineffable;
Because her lips might spill a kiss
That, dripping in a world like this,
Would tincture death's myrrh-bitter stream
To sweetness—so I called her "Dream."

"DREAM"

Because I could not understand
The magic touches of a hand
That seemed, beneath her strange control,
To smooth the plumage of the soul
And calm it, till, with folded wings,
It half forgot its flutterings,
And, nestled in her palm, did seem
To trill a song that called her "Dream."

Because I saw her, in a sleep
As dark and desolate and deep
And fleeting as the taunting night
That flings a vision of delight
To some lorn martyr as he lies
In slumber ere the day he dies—
Because she vanished like a gleam
Of glory, do I call her "Dream."

A WRANGDILLION

I

DEXERY-TETHERY! down in the dike,
   Under the—Under the ooze and the slime,
Nestles the wraith of a reticent Gryke,
    Blubbering bubbles of rhyme:
Though the reeds touch him and tickle his teeth—
   Though the Grai—Though the Graigroll and
      the Cheest
Pluck at the leaves of his laureate-wreath,
    Nothing affects him the least.

CHORUS

Nay, nothing—Nay, nothing affects him the least!
They may say he sings less like a bird than a beast—
They may say that his song is both patchy and pieced—
That its worst may be his, but the best he has fleeced

A WRANGDILLION

From old dinky masters not only deceased
But damn'd ere their dying,— Yet nothing the least—
Nothing affects him the least!

II

He sinks to the dregs in the dead o' the night,
    And he shuf—And he shuffles the shadows about
As he gathers the stars in a nest of delight
    And sets there and hatches them out:
The Zhederrill peers from his watery mine
    In scorn with—In scorn with the Will-o'-the-wisp,
As he twinkles his eyes in a whisper of shine
    That ends in a luminous lisp.

CHORUS

Nay, nothing—Nay, nothing affects him the least!
They may say he sings less like a bird than a beast—
They may say that his song is both patchy and pieced—
That its worst may be his, but the best he has fleeced
From old dinky masters not only deceased
But damn'd ere their dying,— Yet nothing the least—
Nothing affects him the least!

THE WITCH OF ERKMURDEN

I

WHO cantereth forth in the night so late—
  So late in the night, and so nigh the dawn?
'Tis The Witch of Erkmurden who leapeth the gate
Of the old churchyard where the three Sprites wait
  Till the whir of her broom is gone.

And who peereth down from the belfry tall,
  With the ghost-white face and the ghastly stare,
With lean hands clinched in the grated wall
Where the red vine rasps and the rank leaves fall,
  And the clock-stroke drowns his prayer?

II

The wee babe wails, and the storm grows loud,
  Nor deeper the dark of the night may be,
For the lightning's claw, with a great wet cloud,

THE WITCH OF ERKMURDEN

Hath wiped the moon and the wild-eyed crowd
   Of the stars out wrathfully.

Knuckled and kinked as the hunchback shade
   Of a thorn-tree bendeth the beldam old
Over the couch where the mother-maid,
With her prayerful eyes, and the babe are laid,
   Waiting the doom untold.

"Mother, O Mother, I only crave
   Mercy for him and the babe—not me!"
"Hush! for it maketh my brain to rave
Of my two white shrouds, and my one wide grave,
   And a mound for my children three."

"Mother, O Mother, I only pray
   Pity for him who is son to thee
And more than my brother.—" "Wilt hush, I say!
Though I meet thee not at the Judgment Day,
   I will bury my children three!"

"Then hark! O Mother, I hear his cry—
   Hear his curse from the church-tower now,—

THE WITCH OF ERKMURDEN

'Ride thou witch till thy hate shall die,
Yet hell as heaven eternally
  Be sealed to such as thou!'"

An infant's wail—then a laugh, god wot,
  That strangled the echoes of deepest hell;
And a thousand shuttles of lightning shot,
And the moon bulged out like a great red blot,
  And a shower of blood-stars fell.

III

There is one wide grave scooped under the eaves—
  Under the eaves as they weep and weep;
And, veiled by the mist that the dead storm weaves,
The hag bends low, and the earth receives
  Mother and child asleep.

There's the print of the hand at either throat,
  And the frothy ooze at the lips of each,
But both smile up where the new stars float,
And the moon sails out like a silver boat
  Unloosed from a stormy beach.

IV

Bright was the morn when the sexton gray
  Twirled the rope of the old church-bell,—
But it answered not, and he tugged away—
And lo, at his feet a dead man lay—
  Dropped down with a single knell.

And the scared wight found, in the lean hand gripped,
  A scrip which read: "O the grave is wide,
But it empty waits, for the low eaves dripped
Their prayerful tears, and the three Sprites slipped
  Away with my babe and bride."

LAUGHTER

WITHIN the cosiest corner of my dreams
   He sits, high-throned above all gods that be
   Portrayed in marble-cold mythology,
Since from his joyous eyes a twinkle gleams
So warm with life and light it ever seems
   Spraying in mists of sunshine over me,
   And mingled with such rippling ecstasy
As overleaps his lips in laughing streams.

  Ho! look on him, and say if he be old
Or youthful! Hand in hand with gray old Time
   He toddled when an infant; and, behold!—
He hath not aged, but to the lusty prime
   Of babyhood—his brow a trifle bold—
   His hair a ravelled nimbus of gray gold.

ERE I WENT MAD

Ere I went mad—
O you may never guess what dreams I had!
Such hosts of happy things did come to me.
One time, it seemed, I knelt at some one's knee,
My wee lips threaded with a strand of prayer,
With kinks of kisses in it here and there
To stay and tangle it the while I knit
A mother's long-forgotten name in it.
Be sure, I dreamed it all, but I was glad
—Ere I went mad!

Ere I went mad,
I dreamed there came to me a fair-faced lad,
Who led me by the wrist where blossoms grew
In grassy lands, and where the skies were blue

ERE I WENT MAD

As his own eyes. And he did lisp and sing,
And weave me wreaths where I sat marvelling
What little prince it was that crowned me queen
And caught my face so cunningly between
His dimple-dinted hands, and kept me glad
—Ere I went mad!

Ere I went mad,
Not even winter weather made me sad—
I dreamed, indeed, the skies were ne'er so dull
That *his* smile might not make them beautiful.
And now, it seemed, he had grown O so fair
And straight and strong that, when he smoothed
    my hair,
I felt as any lily with drooped head
That leans, in fields of grain unharvested,
By some lithe stalk of barley—pure and glad
—Ere I went mad!

Ere I went mad,
The last of all the happy dreams I had
Was of a peerless king—a conqueror—

ERE I WENT MAD

Who crowned me with a kiss, and throned me for
One hour! Ah, God of Mercy! what a dream
To tincture life with! Yet I made no scream
As I awakened—with these eyes you see,
That may not smile till love comes back to me,
And lulls me back to those old dreams I had
—Ere I went mad.

ETERNITY

O WHAT a weary while it is to stand,
　Telling the countless ages o'er and o'er,
　Till all the finger-tips held out before
Our dazzled eyes by heaven's starry hand
Drop one by one, yet at some dread command
　Are held again, and counted evermore!
　How feverish the music seems to pour
Along the throbbing veins of anthems grand!
　And how the cherubim sing on and on—
The seraphim and angels—still in white—
　Still harping—still enraptured—far withdrawn
In hovering armies tranced in endless flight!
　. . . God's mercy! is there never dusk or dawn,
　Or any crumb of gloom to feed upon?

THE SPEEDING OF THE KING'S SPITE

A King—estranged from his loving Queen
    By a foolish royal whim—
Tired and sick of the dull routine
    Of matters surrounding him—
Issued a mandate in this wise:—
    " The dower of my daughter's hand
I will give to him who holds this prize,
    The strangest thing in the land."

But the King, sad sooth! in this grim decree
    Had a motive low and mean;—
'Twas a royal piece of chicanery
    To harry and spite the Queen—
For King though he was, and beyond compare,
    He had ruled all things save one—
Then blamed the Queen that his only heir
    Was a daughter—not a son.

THE SPEEDING OF THE KING'S SPITE

The girl had grown, in the mother's care,
   Like a bud in the shine and shower
That drinks of the wine of the balmy air
   Till it blooms into matchless flower;
Her waist was the rose's stem that bore
   The flower—and the flower's perfume—
That ripens on till it bulges o'er
   With its wealth of bud and bloom.

And she had a lover—lowly sprung,—
   But a purer, nobler heart
Never spake in a courtlier tongue
   Or wooed with a dearer art:
And the fair pair paled at the King's decree;
   But the smiling Fates contrived
To have them wed, in a secrecy
   That the Queen *herself* connived—

While the grim King's heralds scoured the land
   And the countries round about,
Shouting aloud, at the King's command,
   A challenge to knave or lout,

THE SPEEDING OF THE KING'S SPITE

Prince or peasant,—"The mighty King
    Would have ye understand
That he who shows him the strangest thing
    Shall have his daughter's hand!"

And thousands flocked to the royal throne,
    Bringing a thousand things
Strange and curious;—One, a bone—
    The hinge of a fairy's wings:
And one, the glass of a mermaid queen,
    Gemmed with a diamond dew,
Where, down in its reflex, dimly seen,
    Her face smiled out at you.

One brought a cluster of some strange date,
    With a subtle and searching tang
That seemed, as you tasted, to penetrate
    The heart like a serpent's fang;
And back you fell for a spell entranced,
    As cold as a corpse of stone,
And heard your brains, as they laughed and danced
    And talked in an undertone.

THE SPEEDING OF THE KING'S SPITE

One brought a bird that could whistle a tune
    So piercingly pure and sweet,
That tears would fall from the eyes of the moon
    In dewdrops at its feet;
And the winds would sigh at the sweet refrain,
    Till they swooned in an ecstasy,
To waken again in a hurricane
    Of riot and jubilee.

One brought a lute that was wro't of a shell
    Luminous as the shine
Of a new-born star in a dewy dell,—
    And its strings were strands of wine
That sprayed at the Fancy's touch and fused,
    As your listening spirit leant
Drunken through with the airs that oozed
    From the o'ersweet instrument.

One brought a tablet of ivory
    Whereon no thing was writ,—
But, at night—and the dazzled eyes would see
    Flickering lines o'er it,—

THE SPEEDING OF THE KING'S SPITE

And each, as you read from the magic tome,
   Lightened and died in flame,
And the memory held but a golden poem
   Too beautiful to name.

Till it seemed all marvels that ever were known
   Or dreamed of under the sun
Were brought and displayed at the royal throne,
   And put by, one by one;—
Till a graybeard monster came to the King—
   Haggard and wrinkled and old—
And spread to his gaze this wondrous thing,—
   A gossamer veil of gold.—

Strangely marvellous—mocking the gaze
   Like a tangle of bright sunshine,
Dipping a million glittering rays
   In a baptism divine:
And a maiden, sheened in this gauze attire—
   Sifting a glance of her eye—
Dazzled men's souls with a fierce desire
   To kiss and caress her and—die.

THE SPEEDING OF THE KING'S SPITE

And the grim King swore by his royal beard
   That the veil had won the prize,
While the gray old monster blinked and leered
   With his lashless, red-rimmed eyes,
As the fainting form of the princess fell,
   And the mother's heart went wild,
Throbbing and swelling a muffled knell
   For the dead hopes of her child.

But her clouded face with a faint smile shone,
   As suddenly, through the throng,
Pushing his way to the royal throne,
   A fair youth strode along,
While a strange smile hovered about his eyes,
   As he said to the grim old King:—
"The veil of gold must lose the prize;
   For *I* have a stranger thing."

He bent and whispered a sentence brief;
   But the monarch shook his head,
With a look expressive of unbelief—
   "It can't be so," he said;

THE SPEEDING OF THE KING'S SPITE

"Or give me proof; and I, the King,
  Give you my daughter's hand,—
For certes THAT *is* a stranger thing—
  The strangest thing in the land!"

Then the fair youth, turning, caught the Queen
  In a rapturous caress,
While his lithe form towered in lordly mien,
  As he said in a brief address:—
"My fair bride's mother is this; and, lo,
  As you stare in your royal awe,
By this pure kiss do I proudly show
  A love for a mother-in-law!"

Then a thaw set in on the old King's mood,
  And a sweet Spring freshet came
Into his eyes, and his heart renewed
  Its love for the favored dame:
But often he has been heard to declare
  That "he never could clearly see
How, in the deuce, such a strange affair
  Could have ended so happily!"

THE ASSASSIN

FLING him amongst the cobbles of the street
   Midmost along a mob's most turbid tide;
   Stun him with tumult upon every side—
Wrangling of hoarsened voices that repeat
His awful guilt and howl for vengeance meet;
   Let white-faced women stare, all torrid-eyed,
   With hair blown forward, and with jaws dropped wide,
And some face like his mother's glimmer sweet
An instant in the hot core of his eyes.
   Then snatch him with claw hands, and thong his head
That he may look no way but toward the skies
   That glower lividly and crackle red,—
There let some knuckled fist of lightning rise—
   Draw backward flickeringly and knock him dead.

A VARIATION

I AM tired of this!
  Nothing else but loving!
Nothing else but kiss and kiss,
  Coo, and turtle-doving!
    Can't you change the order some?
    Hate me just a little—come!

Lay aside your "dears,"
  "Darlings," "kings," and "princes!"—
Call me knave, and dry your tears—
  Nothing in me winces,—
    Call me something low and base—
    Something that will suit the case!

Wish I had your eyes
  And their drooping lashes!
I would dry their teary lies
  Up with lightning-flashes—

A VARIATION

Make your sobbing lips unsheathe
All the glitter of your teeth!

Can't you lift one word—
　With some pang of laughter—
Louder than the drowsy bird
　Crooning 'neath the rafter?
　　Just one bitter word, to shriek
　　Madly at me as I speak!

How I hate the fair
　Beauty of your forehead!
How I hate your fragrant hair!
　How I hate the torrid
　　Touches of your splendid lips,
　　And the kiss that drips and drips!

Ah, you pale at last!
　And your face is lifted
Like a white sail to the blast,
　And your hands are shifted
　　Into fists: and, towering thus,
　　You are simply glorious!

A VARIATION

Now before me looms
   Something more than human;
Something more than beauty blooms
   In the wrath of Woman—
      Something to bow down before
      Reverently and adore.

AN OUT-WORN SAPPHO

How tired I am! I sink down all alone
  Here by the wayside of the Present. Lo,
Even as a child I hide my face and moan—
  A little girl that may no farther go:
  The path above me only seems to grow
    More rugged, climbing still, and ever briered
  With keener thorns of pain than these below;
  And O the bleeding feet that falter so
    And are so very tired!

Why, I have journeyed from the far-off Lands
  Of Babyhood—where baby-lilies blew
Their trumpets in mine ears, and filled my hands
  With treasures of perfume and honey-dew,
  And where the orchard shadows ever drew

AN OUT-WORN SAPPHO

    Their cool arms round me when my cheeks
        were fired
    With too much joy, and lulled mine eyelids to,
    And only let the starshine trickle through
        In sprays, when I was tired!

Yet I remember, when the butterfly
    Went flickering about me like a flame
That quenched itself in roses suddenly,
    How oft I wished that *I* might blaze the same,
    And in some rose-wreath nestle with my name,
        While all the world looked on it and admired.—
    Poor moth!—Along my wavering flight toward
        fame
    The winds drive backward, and my wings are
        lame
        And broken, bruised and tired!

I hardly know the path from those old times;
    I know at first it was a smoother one
Than this that hurries past me now, and climbs
    So high, its far cliffs even hide the sun

AN OUT-WORN SAPPHO

And shroud in gloom my journey scarce begun.
   I could not do quite all the world required—
I could not do quite all I should have done,
And in my eagerness I have outrun
     My strength—and I am tired. . . .

Just tired! But when of old I had the stay
   Of mother-hands, O very sweet indeed
It was to dream that all the weary way
   I should but follow where I now must lead—
   For long ago they left me in my need,
     And, groping on alone, I tripped and mired
   Among rank grasses where the serpents breed
   In knotted coils about the feet of speed.—
     There first it was I tired.

And yet I staggered on, and bore my load
   Right gallantly: The sun, in summer-time,
In lazy belts came slipping down the road
   To woo me on, with many a glimmering rhyme
   Rained from the golden rim of some fair clime,
     That, hovering beyond the clouds, inspired

AN OUT-WORN SAPPHO

My failing heart with fancies so sublime
I half forgot my path of dust and grime,
    Though I was growing tired.

And there were many voices cheering me:
    I listened to sweet praises where the wind
Went laughing o'er my shoulders gleefully
    And scattering my love-songs far behind;—
    Until, at last, I thought the world so kind—
      So rich in all my yearning soul desired—
    So generous—so loyally inclined,
    I grew to love and trust it. . . . I was blind—
      Yea, blind as I was tired!

And yet one hand held me in creature-touch:
    And O, how fain it was, how true and strong,
How it did hold my heart up like a crutch,
    Till, in my dreams, I joyed to walk along
    The toilsome way, contented with a song—
      'Twas all of earthly things I had acquired,
    And 'twas enough, I feigned, or right or wrong,
    Since, binding me to man—a mortal thong—
      It stayed me, growing tired. . . .

AN OUT-WORN SAPPHO

Yea, I had e'en resigned me to the strait
   Of earthly rulership—had bowed my head
Acceptant of the master-mind—the great
   One lover—lord of all,—the perfected
   Kiss-comrade of my soul;—had stammering said
     My prayers to him;—all—all that he desired
   I rendered sacredly as we were wed.—
   Nay—nay!—'twas but a myth I worshippèd.—
     And—God of love!—how tired!

For, O my friends, to lose the latest grasp—
   To feel the last hope slipping from its hold—
To feel the one fond hand within your clasp
   Fall slack, and loosen with a touch so cold
   Its pressure may not warm you as of old
     Before the light of love had thus expired—
   To know your tears are worthless, though they
       rolled
   Their torrents out in molten drops of gold.—
     God's pity! I am tired!

And I must rest.—Yet do not say "She *died*,"
   In speaking of me, sleeping here alone.
I kiss the grassy grave I sink beside,

AN OUT-WORN SAPPHO

And close mine eyes in slumber all mine own:
Hereafter I shall neither sob nor moan
 Nor murmur one complaint;—all I desired,
And failed in life to find, will now be known—
So let me dream. Good night! And on the stone
 Say simply: She was tired.

AFTER DEATH

Ah! this delights me more than words could tell,—
  To just lie stark and still, with folded hands
That tremble not at greeting or farewell,
  Nor fumble foolishly in loosened strands
    Of woman's hair, nor grip with jealousy
    To find her face turned elsewhere smilingly.

With slumbrous lids, and mouth in mute repose,
  And lips that yearn no more for any kiss—
Though it might drip, as from the red-lipped rose
  The dewdrop drips, 'twere not so sweet as this
    Unutterable density of rest
    That reigns in every vein of brain and breast!

And thus—soaked with still laughter through and through—
  I lie here dreaming of the forms that pass

AFTER DEATH

Above my grave, to drop, with tears, a few
  White flowers that but curdle the green
    grass;—
  And if they read such sermons, they could see
  How I do pity them that pity me.

TO THE WINE-GOD MERLUS

[*A Toast of Jucklet's*]

Ho! ho! thou jolly god, with kinkèd lips
And laughter-streaming eyes, thou liftest up
The heart of me like any wassail-cup,
And from its teeming brim, in foaming drips,
Thou blowest all my cares. I cry to thee,
Between the sips:—Drink long and lustily;
Drink thou my ripest joys, my richest mirth,
My maddest staves of wanton minstrelsy;
Drink every song I've tinkered here on earth
With any patch of music; drink! and be
Thou drainer of my soul, and to the lees
Drink all my lover-thrills and ecstasies;
And with a final gulp—ho! ho!—drink me,
And roll me o'er thy tongue eternally.

THE QUEST

I AM looking for Love. Has he passed this way,
With eyes as blue as the skies of May,
And a face as fair as the summer dawn?—
You answer back, but I wander on,—
For you say: "Oh, yes; but his eyes were gray,
And his face as dim as a rainy day."

Good friends, I query, I search for Love;
His eyes are as blue as the skies above,
And his smile as bright as the midst of May
When the truce-bird pipes: Has he passed this way?
And one says: "Ay; but his face, alack!
Frowned as he passed, and his eyes were black."

O who will tell me of Love? I cry!
His eyes are as blue as the mid-May sky,

THE QUEST

And his face as bright as the morning sun;
And you answer and mock me, every one,
That his eyes were dark, and his face was wan,
And he passed you frowning and wandered on.

But stout of heart will I onward fare,
Knowing *my* Love is beyond—somewhere,—
The Love I seek, with the eyes of blue,
And the bright, sweet smile unknown of you;
And on from the hour his trail is found
I shall sing sonnets the whole year round.

SONG OF PARTING

Say farewell, and let me go:
  Shatter every vow!
All the future can bestow
  Will be welcome now!
    And if this fair hand I touch
    I have worshipped overmuch,
    It was my mistake—and so,
    Say farewell, and let me go.

Say farewell, and let me go:
  Murmur no regret,
Stay your tear-drops ere they flow—
  Do not waste them yet!
    They might pour as pours the rain,
    And not wash away the pain:—
    I have tried them and I know.—
    Say farewell, and let me go.

SONG OF PARTING

Say farewell, and let me go:
   Think me not untrue—
True as truth is, even so
    I am true to you!
      If the ghost of love may stay
      Where my fond heart dies to-day,
      I am with you alway—so,
      Say farewell, and let me go.

THREE SEVERAL BIRDS

The Romancer, the Poet, and the Bookman

I

THE ROMANCER

THE Romancer's a nightingale,—
  The moon wanes dewy-dim
And all the stars grow faint and pale
  In listening to him.—
To him the plot least plausible
  Is of the most avail,—
He simply masters it because
  He takes it by the tale.

> *O he's a nightingale,—*
> *His theme will never fail—*
> *It gains applause of all—because*
> *He takes it by the tale!*

THREE SEVERAL BIRDS

The Romancer's a nightingale:—
   His is the sweetest note—
The sweetest, woe-begonest wail
   Poured out of mortal throat:
So, glad or sad, he ever draws
   Our best godspeed and hail;
He highest lifts his theme—because
   He takes it by the tale.

O he's a nightingale,—
His theme will never fail—
It gains applause of all—because
He takes it by the tale!

II

THE POET

The bobolink he sings a single song,
               Right along,—
And the robin sings another, all his own—
               One alone;

THREE SEVERAL BIRDS

And the whippoorwill, and bluebird,
And the cockadoodle-doo-bird;—
But the mocking-bird he sings in every tone
                     Ever known,
Or chirrup-note of merriment or moan.

So the Poet he's the mocking-bird of men,—
*He steals his songs and sings them o'er **again;***
  And yet beyond believing
    They're the sweeter for his thieving.—
So we'll howl for Mister Mocking-bird
  And have him out again!

It's mighty fond we are of bobolinks,
                     And chewinks;
And we dote on dinky robins, quite a few—
                     Yes, we do;
And we love the dove, and bluebird,
And the cockadoodle-doo-bird,—
But the mocking-bird's the bird for me and you,
                     Through and through,
Since he sings as everybody wants him to.

THREE SEVERAL BIRDS

Ho! the Poet he's the mocking-bird of men,—
He steals his songs and sings them o'er again;
And yet beyond believing
They're the sweeter for his thieving.—
So we'll howl for Mister Mocking-bird
And have him out again!

III

BOOKMAN'S CATCH

The Bookman he's a humming-bird—
  His feasts are honey-fine,—
    (With hi! hilloo!
    And clover-dew
  And roses lush and rare!)
His roses are the phrase and word
  Of olden tomes divine;
    (With hi! and ho!
    And pinks ablow
  And posies everywhere!)
The Bookman he's a humming-bird,—
  He steals from song to song—

THREE SEVERAL BIRDS

He scents the ripest-blooming rhyme,
   And takes his heart along
And sacks all sweets of bursting verse
   And ballads, throng on throng.
      (With ho! and hey!
      And brook and brae,
      And brinks of shade and shine!)

A humming-bird the Bookman is—
   Though cumbrous, gray and grim,—
      (With hi! hilloo!
      And honey-dew
      And odors musty-rare!)
He bends him o'er that page of his
   As o'er the rose's rim.
      (With hi! and ho!
      And pinks aglow
      And roses everywhere!)
Ay, he's the featest humming-bird,—
   On airiest of wings
He poises pendent o'er the poem
   That blossoms as it sings—

THREE SEVERAL BIRDS

God friend him as he dips his beak
  In such delicious things!
      (With ho! and hey!
     And world away
   And only dreams for him!)